I'M
ONLY IN IT
FOR THE
PARKING

www.**penguin**.co.uk

I'M ONLY IN IT FOR THE PARKING

Everything I know about life, laughter and disability

Lee Ridley
AKA
LOST VOICE GUY

CORGI BOOKS

TRANSWORLD PUBLISHERS
Penguin Random House, One Embassy Gardens,
8 Viaduct Gardens, London SW11 7BW
www.penguin.co.uk

Transworld is part of the Penguin Random House group of companies
whose addresses can be found at global.penguinrandomhouse.com

Penguin
Random House
UK

First published in Great Britain in 2019 by Bantam Press
an imprint of Transworld Publishers
Corgi edition published 2021

A CIP catalogue record for this book
is available from the British Library.

ISBN 9780552176323

Typeset in 11.16/15pt Dante MT Std
by Integra Software Services Pvt. Ltd, Pondicherry.

Printed and bound in Great Britain by Clays Ltd, Elcograf S.p.A.

The authorized representative in the EEA is Penguin Random House Ireland,
Morrison Chambers, 32 Nassau Street, Dublin D02 YH68.

Penguin Random House is committed to a sustainable future
for our business, our readers and our planet. This book is
made from Forest Stewardship Council® certified paper.

This book is dedicated to my wonderful mam and dad, Janet and David, also my sister, Nicola, and brother-in-law, Jonathan, and my adorable niece, Charlotte.

Without their love and support, I wouldn't have had the amazing adventures I've had, and this book wouldn't have been possible. Oh, and they've featured in a fair few embarrassing stories in it as well. Sorry about that.

Thank you from the bottom of my heart for being who you are.

CONTENTS

Foreword

MEET NON-SPEAKING MAN

Of course Lost Voice Guy isn't my real name. My parents were never mean enough to put that on my birth certificate. At least, that's what they told me to say whenever the nice person from Social Services visited. That's a joke, by the way. I feel I have to point this out to you just in case Social Services actually decide to pay my parents a visit regarding the historic mistreatment of their son. Yeah . . . *finally* responding to that call I put in back in 1990.

Lost Voice Guy is a stage name I gave myself to stand out from the crowd. Let's face it, when you're on a bill with ten other comedians, it's a lot easier to remember Lost Voice Guy than it is to remember some random name . . . Well, it should be. Though I'll also answer to 'No Voice Boy', 'Non-Speaking Man', 'Voiceless Bloke' and 'Him who won *The X Factor*'.

I use a stage name because I felt I had to be upfront about my disability. I didn't want it to be the elephant in the room as I was walking out onstage . . . and I didn't want it to distract people from my actual material. There's nothing worse than facing a crowd who are feeling awkward or who aren't sure whether to laugh or not. By calling myself Lost Voice Guy I was putting all my cards on the table and saying: 'Yes, this is who I am and, yes, I have a disability. The clue is in the name.'

I want people to realize straight away that I'm comfortable to joke about my condition (my range of T-shirts helps with this) and therefore, hopefully, make them fine with it, like I'm fine with it. I'm not there to be a freak show. I don't want anybody's pity. I'm just there to have a laugh and help everyone have a good time. That's also the reason why I usually open most of my sets with a few quick-fire gags about my disability. I've always found it helps put people at ease and then I can get on with the business of making them laugh.

So, my real name is Lee, and I've been disabled since before it was popular.

I wasn't born this way. In fact, I was a fit and healthy young lad until I was six months old. Then I developed sores in my mouth and fell very unwell. According to my mam, over the next few days my condition worsened, my temperature remained high and my mouth was so sore that I wasn't able to feed properly. Worrying times, as you can imagine. But it got worse. I then started convulsing and was admitted to hospital. Over the next few days I had various tests, including a brain scan, which suggested I might have a tumour. By this time I was becoming comatose. Never a good sign, and I'm no doctor. Further investigation revealed that I had developed encephalitis.

Eventually the treatment I received was effective in treating my condition, but it left me with a right-sided weakness, which was – and is – similar to a stroke in its effects. That's why I move like a zombie out of *The Walking Dead* – because the right side of my body is weaker than my left. It's also why I can't do a lot of things that most other people take for granted. I can't walk in a straight line, for example. I've tried. On a number of occasions. But the more I try to walk straight, the more wonky my walk becomes. It's like those times when you're trying to convince the bouncer you're not drunk so they'll let you into a club. No one's falling for it. I did once try to get completely off my face in the hope that if I drank enough I'd walk straight, but it just gave me a bladder infection. During my drinking binge, I did think about going to Alcoholics Anonymous, but I was worried that I'd have trouble with the Twelve Steps. Another little joke there.

That's right, stairs are a struggle too (one of the many things that the Daleks and I have in common). I can't manage them at all unless there's a handrail – ideally on my left-hand side – or something or someone else to grab on to as I go up and down. It goes without saying that escalators are totally off limits. If I can't deal with stairs that don't move, then I'm fucked with stairs that do. Although I remember once as a brave teenager I stood at the top of the escalator attempting to coordinate my already shaky leg movements with the rhythm of the escalator stairs. After fifteen minutes, I gave up and went to find the lift.

Neither can I walk long distances without getting really tired. It wasn't always this bad. When I was younger I used to be able to walk quite a way, but it's got worse over the years . . . mostly because I'm an old bastard now. A thirty-eight-year-old bastard, to be precise. These days I usually rely on a wheelchair, mobility scooter or taxi if I'm going further than fifty metres. I do still like to walk when I can, though. I need a bit of help but I'm stubborn enough to try my best. My wonky legs have served me well for this long, so I'm not letting them give up now.

My general physical movements are also pretty restricted. I'm shit at bending down and picking up stuff off the floor (so I can't shop at Primark) or at reaching up and getting anything off a high shelf (so I can't buy any porn). As long as I shop where everything is at eye level I'm sorted.

So, that's my body.

I use a communication aid to speak. I actually use an app on the iPad to do my talking at the moment, but over the years I've had many different devices of varying shapes and sizes (though I'm glad to say the general trend is that they've been getting smaller) – enough to open a museum if only I'd kept them all.

Because my illness developed within the first year of my life, I'm classed as having cerebral palsy. As a kid, it was never really explained what had happened to me, probably because the doctors didn't have Google in those days. Needless to say, when I found out I'd never be able to talk again, I was speechless.

On the upside, Lost Voice Guy was born.

UK ADULT MALE GRAHAM

1

A lot of water had to pass under the Tyne Bridge before I could go from being a Geordie kid with a disabled parking badge to seeing how much I could get away with taking the piss out of Simon Cowell on national TV without spoiling my chances of winning *Britain's Got Talent*. (Quite a lot, as it turned out.) What happened and when, how and even why – with a bit of wow thrown in – is what this book is about. But before we can get properly under way, my voice app has a few announcements to make.

I've lived in Newcastle all my life, but for some reason I still haven't picked up the accent. In fact, if you're struggling to place my distinctive mode of address, that's because it's from PC World. People often wonder why I chose to use such a posh voice for my talker. Let's be honest, it wouldn't be out of place reading the shipping forecast on Radio 4. The fact is that I simply didn't have much choice in the matter. The option I selected is called UK Adult Male Graham and it's one of the few voices available to me. Some of my other options are:

- A British female voice – which I use on Tuesday nights when I like to put on something silky
- A little boy's voice – this is just creepy
- A little girl's voice – creepier still, but good to use when you want to mess with cold callers
- An American male voice – but Donald Trump's ruined the idea of pretending to be an all-American hero. Not a good time to be American
- An Arabic male voice – I'm dying to use this one but I'm not sure if it'd be racist. After all, I own the voice so I should be allowed to use it, but I don't think a white British male would get away with that excuse. I'm pretty sure I'd be called out for cultural appropriation but a part of me still thinks, Why the hell not?
- An Australian male voice – for when I finally get the part on *Neighbours* that I've wanted since I was a kid
- An old man's voice – probably as creepy as the kids' voices but for entirely different reasons. Let's just say I can never say, 'Do you want to come and see my puppy?' using it. People would flinch
- A happy man's voice – for when Newcastle win a match
- A sad man's voice – for when Newcastle lose a match. This one is used much more regularly
- A hip-hop male adult voice – which, as a white man who can't jump, I could never pull off

- Yoda's voice – yes, that's right, I can, if I choose, sound like Yoda from *Star Wars*. For fun, I do sometimes so choose
- Queen Elizabeth II's voice – I can also inexplicably sound like the Queen. This is just weird

I'm not quite sure why the last two options exist. Before I had the choice, I'd certainly never felt the need to sound like either Yoda or the Queen. But now I have it, I'm strangely drawn to using both from time to time. I suspect you would, too, if you could. But, as far as adult male voices go, good old UK Adult Male Graham was my best option . . . even if he does sound like he should be telling a children's story on *Jackanory* . . . I could be on to something there if the stand-up ever goes down the pan.

If you're wondering whether I think in my UK Adult Male Graham voice, then let me tell you I don't. I hope that answer hasn't come as a surprise. I doubt that many people sound the same in their own head as they do out loud, but it goes without saying – doesn't it? – that this is especially the case for me. I have an actual voice called Graham and I also have a head voice, which is most definitely Lee, and the two are very different. I might not have a regional accent for my talker just yet, but in my head I sound as Geordie as the talented one out of Ant and Dec (whichever one he may be, I couldn't possibly say). I'm as local as the cast of *Geordie Shore* . . . just not as drunk, despite appearances. While I might type 'get lost', I really mean 'haddaway'. If I'm on my way home, I'm really 'gannin' hyem'. And when I say, 'Yes', I definitely mean 'Why aye, man!' Despite not having the accent, I'm proud to be a Geordie.

The real question is which voice are you hearing when you read this book? Are you hearing the words in my UK Adult Male Graham actual voice? Or are you hearing them in my 'as Geordie as Sting used to be before he went all posh' head voice? Or maybe you're hearing the words in your own voice or another voice entirely? Queen Elizabeth II or Yoda, maybe?

While you think about that for a moment, and give yourself a headache, it's worth saying that I'm not even sure if I'd like a Geordie accent for my talker. In much the same way that Stephen Hawking's voice identified him, my UK Adult Male Graham voice is as much a part of my stand-up now as my humour, T-shirts and facial expressions. And my current posh English accent definitely makes my jokes funnier, especially when I make it swear or read excerpts from *Fifty Shades of Grey*.

It's not that I don't like my talker voice, because I do. I've used it for so long now that I identify it as *my* voice, even though thousands of other disabled people use it (just don't get us all in a room together: that would be very confusing), and I have changed voices at certain points in my life. I dread to think what the voice on my first talker was like when I was eight. Technology being what it was back then, I probably sounded like something out of a bad 1980s sci-fi movie. But as technology has improved, so has my voice . . . thankfully. And, as attached as I am to Graham, I'm not going to count out changing it again in the future.

Looking at it from a technological point of view, it's possible for me to have a Geordie accent if I want one. I'd just need a Geordie bloke to record all the different sounds we make when we speak and someone to work their magic on the computer to put it all together. I'm making it sound simple when it really isn't, but you get the idea.

Who's to say I have to have a Geordie accent at all? I could sound like a sexy Irish bloke, an attractive, rugged Scottish guy . . . or a Scouser. Okay, maybe I won't go for a Scouse accent. But, when you think about it, I could sound like anyone I fancy. Most people don't get to choose their voice – David Beckham would probably like to swap his for something a little more resonant. But I've made a list of people I'd be happy to sound like and perhaps David and I can swap notes:

- Brian Blessed
- Morgan Freeman
- Liam Neeson (okay, maybe not so much him, now)
- Samuel L. Jackson
- George Clooney
- Homer Simpson
- Will Smith
- *The X Factor* voiceover guy
- Reginald D. Hunter

Just for the record, I'm writing this book using my . . .

GEORDIE HEAD VOICE

I have to admit that it's very weird but nonetheless enjoyable for me to be communicating in purely written form. I think one of the reasons I like doing stand-up is because people have to sit there and listen to me without answering back (unless there's a hen party in and they're being incredibly annoying). Mostly when I'm onstage I feel like people finally want to listen to what I have to say. This book is the same in that my thoughts are delivered fully formed and you can't interrupt me. I suppose you can close the book and put it aside, get up and walk away – it's less rude to do that at home than if you were in a small stand-up comedy club and I can see you losing interest.

In a way it's quite nice to be able to talk to you without hearing my UK Adult Male Graham. My real voice is my head voice, the one that I hear every day of my life but the one you'll probably never hear. I write using my head voice. And, on the page, I can get all of my thoughts over to you. This rarely happens in real life because of the delay between me having a thought and typing it out on my talker. I often want to say something but the moment passes before I've had the chance to say it . . . although, on the upside, the time lag has definitely saved me from getting into arguments and having my head kicked in on numerous occasions. All that typing just isn't worth the hassle. And even if I wanted to, I couldn't sound angry anyway. My actual voice is very monotone.

The most difficult time for this is when I'm in a big group of people, all of whom have something to say. It's easier in small groups because I can usually spot when a gap in the conversation is coming up and get ready to say something myself. In bigger groups this is almost impossible.

It's extremely frustrating having something to say and not being able to say it. Of course I've learned to adapt. For example, I sometimes talk using short sentences because I don't get the opportunity to type a lot before the conversation has moved on. Sometimes I end up using hand gestures and facial expressions to communicate because it's simpler than trying to metaphorically shout over other people. I have thought of implementing a system where everyone shuts their gobs when I make some sort of hand signal to allow me to speak, but that sounds a bit too dictator-ish.

At times, I'm guilty of letting other people talk for me. I know this is a bad habit and I'd encourage anyone in a similar situation to try to avoid doing it because it won't help you in the long run. If you don't learn how to communicate well, you can't make friends or hold down a job. But sometimes it's just quicker and easier to let someone else do the talking for you. I've learned to observe, and to join in when I can.

As for the machinery which has helped me get my point across when the opportunity has arisen, it's come in various shapes and sizes and has had many different names over the years – including Touch Talker and Lightwriter. So, to make it simpler for everyone – and because I didn't get around to setting up any kind of sponsorship deal before I started writing this book – I will refer to it here simply as my 'talker'. Although if Apple are reading this, I'll gladly refer to it as my 'amazing talking iPad' in future, if you want to get in touch.

My talker and I have always had a very special relationship. It's almost as if it's a part of me now. I don't even notice it's there when I'm carrying it around, like an extra limb that dangles from my arm. I've even given it a name – Kit, after the car out of *Knight Rider*, for obvious reasons. I never go anywhere without it because I'd be up Shit Creek if I couldn't communicate. We have a love/hate relationship. It's great when it works but it's crap when it doesn't.

Like any technology, it does fuck up sometimes. Like it's trying to remind me of how lucky I am to have it and that I should be more grateful. It's an absolute nightmare when it decides not to work, especially as it tends to happen suddenly and without warning. If this happens I obviously switch it off and switch it back on again as this has fixed every technological malfunction at some point. That's Plan A. If that doesn't work, Plan B is to panic.

Imagine suddenly having your voice taken away for no apparent reason for an unspecified amount of time and not being able to communicate effectively. That's what it's like for me every time my talker decides it doesn't want to play ball. No matter how many times it's happened, the sick feeling I get in my stomach when I realize I'm truly without a voice never gets any easier to deal with. Technology like this isn't something you can fix straight away either. You can't just pop into one of those dodgy backstreet phone-repair shops and ask them to sort it out for twenty quid. It usually requires my talker to be sent away to be fixed by professionals, which means losing my voice for a week or so at least.

Over the years this has meant that I have learned (the hard way) to have back-up plans in place. Although some of these pieces of kit (no pun intended) are pretty expensive, I always make sure I have a substitute in case my main talker decides to go haywire. I'm lucky enough to be in a position to do this. Other people aren't so fortunate. Which is why I wish this technology didn't have to be so expensive. Of course, having a substitute talker at home isn't much good when I'm out and about and my main one decides to break or run out of battery (okay, I hold my hands up on this last point: this is something I should probably manage better).

One of the most memorable times this happened, I was out with my mates and chatting up some girls in a club. All of a sudden my talker died and left me speechless. I knew I had two options. I could try to use gestures in the hope they'd understand me, but I've never chatted anyone up by playing charades before and this seemed like a bad time to start. So, I ended up trying to chat them up by typing on my phone, then passing the screen around to everyone in turn to read. Unsurprisingly, it didn't have the same effect and – what were the odds? – I didn't get lucky that night. It was probably just as well, as I don't know the sign language for any dirty talk in bed. Well, not much anyway!

All of my talkers have taken a bit of time to get used to, even though I like to think of myself as being quite tech-savvy. I've had about five different variations over the years, and whenever a new one comes along it's just like when you get a new phone and don't know how to use it: you end up sexting your grandma instead of your girlfriend. Only in my case, I ended up pressing the wrong button and telling my grandma, to her face: 'You look very hot.'

I've never quite managed to master the volume controls on any of my talkers. I usually find myself shouting something really personal (train journeys are especially bad for this) or murmuring something really important. I long for the day when they introduce a whisper mode into the settings menu.

To be fair to my talker, it works perfectly most of the time, and it does have to put up with lots of rubbish from me. I'm forever dropping it or spilling food or drink on it. I'm amazed it still decides to work for me as much as it does. If I were my talker, I'd have given up on our relationship a long time ago and found someone who treated me much better.

There are rights and wrongs on both sides in pretty much every relationship, though – even Mike Ashley's with Newcastle. And looking at the long-term grievances from my side of the pillow (the one I share with my talker: I'm definitely not sleeping with Mike Ashley), 'Pronunciation Problems' would have to come quite high on the list.

EXCUSE ME?

My talker can pronounce some words better than others, which can get very annoying at times. The best example of this flaw is that it can't say 'lasagne' properly. First World problems, I know. But it just so happens that lasagne is my favourite dish. So, whenever I go to an Italian restaurant, it can take half an hour to order my food because the poor waiter can't understand my talker. I've solved the problem by pointing at the menu instead – it's the traditional English way of reaching out across a language barrier (well, for those of us who can't shout). Most of the time we get there in the end, but I'm never tempted to choose tiramisu for dessert.

This gap between what's in my head as I type and what my talker actually says can cause embarrassment, most notably when I tried to buy the new Jay-Z album from HMV a few years ago. It's hard to find anything in those places at the best of times, which may be one reason why that chain has recently been experiencing the worst, and I spent quite a while looking for his new album. In the end, I decided it would be easier to go up to the counter and ask where it was. An attractive young woman was working that day so obviously I went and asked her. I'm only human. For some strange reason – a recent blow to the head, perhaps – I thought we might connect over our mutual respect for Jay-Z and live happily ever after.

In hindsight, talking to her was a big mistake. Instead of asking my future wife where the new Jay-Z album was, my talker decided to pronounce it 'Jay Zed'. My face turned bright red as she tried to suppress a laugh. (Laughing at the disabled is rarely a good look in retail, or indeed anywhere, unless you're a Donald Trump voter.) I tried to correct myself and spelled out 'Jay Zee' so that I'd say it properly, but the damage was done. I did eventually find the Jay-Z album, but I never got the sales assistant's number and I never went into that branch of HMV again. Don't get me started on how my talker pronounces 'Kanye West' . . .

At other times, it manages to pronounce words correctly but says them in a really weird way. Like when your satnav can't quite say the name of a certain place, but tries its best anyway. Prime examples of this are 'Weetabix' and 'hippo'. If you ever meet me in the street, I'd encourage you to make me say these words, because they do sound pretty funny. Of course, all my mates think it's hilarious when I have to venture into either of these problematic verbal areas and they'll try to get me to say them at every available opportunity.

'What did you have for breakfast, Lee?'

'I know what you're doing, and I'm not being your performing monkey.'

'I'm just asking what you had for breakfast!'

'No, you're not . . .'

'Go on, say it!'

'No!'

'Do it!'

'No!'

'If you don't say it, I'm not going to ring up and order your Jay-Z tickets for you.'

'Fine! I had WEET. A. BIX.' With the *a* as in 'jay'.

At which point, my mates usually roll around the floor laughing their heads off. It works every time. Sometimes if they're feeling really mischievous, they'll take my talker away from me and just start typing stuff themselves. My mates are dickheads sometimes.

TOO FREQUENTLY ASKED QUESTIONS

Of course, what you're happy to accept from your mates and what you're willing to put up with from complete strangers are two very different things. As a disabled person, I get asked lots of stupid questions. It's as if people I've never met before think it's perfectly acceptable to ask me anything they like, that somehow it's their right to know things about me and my disability, and no matter what they say, it couldn't possibly be offensive. They wade right in.

And sometimes it's fine – in this as in all situations I reckon you can tell pretty quickly if someone basically means you well and has just misjudged the situation. But sometimes people aren't just innocently getting it wrong. Their underlying assumptions are incredibly offensive – to the extent that it almost feels like they're doing it just to put me in my place.

Assuming you're someone (as most people are) who basically just wants to do the right thing but isn't sure how – the kind of person where the last thing you want to do is get yourself mixed up in the conversational equivalent of the dark web – I've decided to punctuate this book with a list of the top questions I would very much like never to be asked again. Consider it a public service to disabled and non-disabled people alike. And perhaps a profound and lasting contribution to the sum of human happiness. You're welcome.

Okay, maybe that's putting it a bit strongly, but from a selfish point of view, if even one person reads this and as a consequence decides not to press the Too Frequently Asked Questions button next time they're introduced to a disabled person, my work here will not have been in vain. Especially if the person at the other end of that judiciously abandoned conversational gambit turns out to be me.

To give you some idea of the kind of thing I'm talking about, people often ask, 'What is it like living with cerebral palsy?' as though it's a flatmate I can't get rid of. Maybe they think cerebral palsy is just one of a number of co-habitees I could have lived with and that I chose it over the others. Spina bifida? No, don't much fancy the look of that. Muscular dystrophy? Quite like the sound of it but, no, in the end it's not for me . . .

To be honest, I've had my fair share of shit flatmates – some have been loud, some have been messy, and one has even been a Sunderland supporter – but those key elements of free will and alternative options, which enable you to either evict them or go and live somewhere else, just don't come into play with a lifelong medical condition.

'So, what's it like? You know . . . being disabled?'

I find this question ridiculous because I've lived with my disability for most of my life, so I don't really know any different. It's just like you not knowing how it feels to be you. If I were to ask you how it feels to be able-bodied – assuming that's what you are – what would you say?

You'd say, 'It feels like *this*. It's just how it is. It's me.'

Or 'What does it feel like to be a woman?'

'Well, it feels like *this*.'

Which isn't very helpful. But that's all you know.

So, if I had to give an answer, I would have to say that it's a right pain in the arse . . . and my legs . . . and my back . . . and everywhere else for that matter . . . Maybe it's time I asked cerebral palsy to move out of my flat.

I never really give much thought to my disability until someone else brings it up. It's just normal to me. In fact, I don't think I realized I *was* different when I was really young. Little kids tend to have that sweet innocence about them. They're very loving and non-judgemental, and just get on with their own little lives, and I was treated as any other kid at nursery.

It was only when I got a bit older that I started to notice more that I wasn't quite like most other kids. Luckily by then – thanks to the loving home in which I was raised – I was pretty happy with myself, so being disabled wasn't that big a deal to me. I went to schools for disabled children for most of my childhood and I think this had a bearing on that sense of self and my generally high confidence levels. I grew up around kids with similar conditions to mine, so I didn't see my cerebral palsy as being an issue. I was happy just getting on with life.

All that said, obviously my disability is hard to cope with at times, but maybe not for the reasons you might think. I'm used to not being able to talk. I'm used to walking funny. And I'm used to people thinking I'm deaf and dim, and feeling the need to write everything down for me or shout at me for no reason whatsoever. Maybe I should say something when that sort of thing happens, when people get it completely wrong – it's the only way people are going to learn how to cope at talking with a disabled person – but I usually don't. It's just too awkward and I'm not a fan of making things any more awkward than they already are.

It does amaze me that some people still think we all need to be treated in the same way, regardless of the disability we have. I'm coming across as a really unreasonable and demanding person here, but as a general rule I don't blame people for their mistakes. For the most part, they're not doing it on purpose, they're just being thoughtless. They haven't thought it through. They're just part of a society that doesn't understand disability very well yet. For an individual's attitude to change, society's attitude needs to change first.

And it is changing. Just not as fast as many of us would like. Twenty years ago few were giving a thought to having accessible hotel rooms or making shops more user-friendly for disabled customers. And even ten years ago, the Paralympics were just an afterthought. I certainly don't remember seeing much disabled sport on the television or reported in the newspapers as a kid.

Looking back at it now, this lack of positive role models affected me more than I understood when I was growing up. I didn't see a bright future for myself and I suspect my parents felt the same. It was almost as if disabled people had to be kept in their disabled backwater and they weren't allowed to push into the mainstream. They were allowed to exist but only in the way that the broader society wanted them to exist – with a label saying 'disabled'. I felt as if I wasn't allowed to have ambitions or dreams and that I should just be glad to have what I had, that it was audacious and even irresponsible to ask for more.

Everything felt so separate. We went to separate schools, had our own special doctors, and only rarely did we get to mix with so-called normal kids in any true sense. The last ten years have seen some fantastic leaps forward. But we've also taken several steps back. We've made some progress, but there's still a long way to go.

MY FAMILY AND OTHER GEORDIES

2

was born and grew up in a place called Shotley Bridge in Consett. Admittedly that doesn't make me a true Geordie, but saying that I'm from Newcastle is easier than trying to explain where the hell Shotley Bridge is. In fact, we lived on the same road as Shotley Bridge Hospital, which turned out to be very handy as I seemed to spend quite a lot of time there as a kid.

The fact that I can still remember the layout of its Accident and Emergency Department tells its own story about how many visits I paid them. Mostly it was with a broken head. You know what kids can be like. Always running around and trying to have fun. And despite not being able to run very well, I was no different. It was just that in my case, I didn't stay upright as much as the other kids . . . and since I have no reflexes I could never put my hands out to stop myself falling. Meaning that my head took the brunt of the injuries.

Some of my earliest scars have stayed with me. Like some sort of scar scrapbook that covers my head. I can still remember where most of them came from and it makes a great ice-breaker at social gatherings. The fact of the matter is that I seem to have this amazing ability to trip over anything and everything . . . especially fresh air. I've lost count of the times that I've literally fallen over nothing. It's like my body has just decided that it should mix it up a bit and make me horizontal instead of vertical for a while. As superhero abilities go, it's a pretty shit one, and it's very embarrassing too. So never ask me about all the marks on my head or you'll be there all night. On the bright side, the ladies seem to dig the scars, so maybe it was worth it.

It probably didn't help that my house in Shotley Bridge backed on to a massive garden and there were some woods at the end of it. As a boy, with not many friends living near by, I loved going exploring in those woods. That was the place where I could let my imagination run wild. A kid's mind is an amazing place. I would often imagine that all the other creatures in the wood could talk to me and I had some amazing conversations with them. You would not believe some of the shit Mr Hedgehog got up to. Strangely enough, they all seemed to shut up when I inevitably tripped over a branch, fell over and couldn't call for help.

Those were the days when talkers didn't exist, and saying, 'Help!' in sign language didn't really have the desired effect. It was often left to the family's Old English Sheepdogs, called Ben and Mop, to sniff me out and raise the alarm. In fact, I think the main reason my family moved house was to make sure I didn't end up lost for ever in those woods and being brought up by the animals like some sort of disabled Mowgli.

We moved to Medomsley in County Durham and the family home has been there ever since. It was my dad who built our house. Not on his own, obviously. He did have some help. But he did the majority of the work. My dad is one of those people who always likes to have a project on the go. Other than me, that is. In fact, since building the family home, he's worked on two other houses as well. Having a dad who was very good at DIY was really handy.

LIFE ON MARS

Another asset I could call upon as a child was that, until he retired, my dad used to work for Mars. I mean the chocolate company, not the planet (although that would have been equally amazing). I've always been a big fan of the author Roald Dahl. I still have copies of nearly all of his books. One of my favourites was *Charlie and the Chocolate Factory*. That was what it was like for me growing up. I didn't have small orange people running around the house (apparently one is now the president of the USA), but we certainly had an unlimited supply of chocolate. A garageful, in fact.

My dad was a regional manager, which meant he went around setting up displays of chocolate in shops. It also meant he got to bring some home. Most kids would have loved this but, to be honest – and, hopefully, without being too disloyal – I preferred Cadbury's chocolate. But my mates certainly enjoyed coming around to the house to explore our cave of chocolate. Naturally I used it to my advantage to become one of the most popular kids at school. It turns out that almost anyone can be bribed with a bit of chocolate. One kid even scored an own goal in a game of football, allowing my team to win, because I'd promised him a bag of sweets afterwards. I reckon he now works for the FA.

I've always considered the house in Medomsley to be my proper home. While I might have been born in Shotley Bridge, I was mostly too young to remember much about the place. I can remember the important stuff, like Christmases, birthdays, falling down and cracking my head open, but the majority of my childhood memories were made in Medomsley.

Considering I was disabled, our house wasn't adapted for my specific needs. It was just a normal house. When I go back now I struggle with the stairs a bit, but back then I seemed to manage fine. Probably another sign that I'm getting a bit old.

The house in Medomsley also had a big garden. In fact, it was big enough for me to have my own mini football pitch with two sets of goals at each end. Some of my favourite memories are of playing football with my grandad on that grass on warm summer days. Even when I didn't have anyone else to play with, I still went out and played football against myself. Letting my imagination run wild again.

I had to make my own entertainment because Medomsley is a very quiet village. Apart from a youth club in the church hall once a week, there wasn't really much to do. And even when I did go to the youth club, I was way too shy to interact with many of the other kids. My disability and lack of self-confidence held me back too much. My dad did once promise to put up a Scalextric track in our house, so that I'd have a bit of entertainment, but I'm still waiting thirty years later.

It was quite hard growing up in a quiet village when I was already feeling very isolated. I think that's the main reason why I didn't stick around in Medomsley much after I came back from university. Medomsley is a beautiful place to live but, after tasting the city life, it was too quiet for me.

I was around dogs as much as people when I was younger, which is probably why I'm still a dog person now. My family have always had dogs. Ben and Mop were first, then came Donald and Philip, then George, the last three all Labradors. In case you're wondering, their names have been changed to protect their identities (and also my internet passwords). And despite most of them getting too excited, jumping up at me and knocking me over on a regular basis, I just adored having a dog around the house. Someone else who couldn't talk – no wonder we got on so well! I always had a sense that our dogs knew I was a bit different and I can't help feeling that they looked out for me more as a consequence. Either way, it was nice to have a dog with me when I was feeling a bit lonely.

Another thing that sticks in my mind about growing up in Medomsley is the amount of snow we had during winter. It's a running joke in the North East that even during the height of summer it's probably still snowing in Medomsley. For a disabled bloke, having to deal with so much snow every year was an absolute nightmare. For a start, it meant that I was stuck inside even more than usual. There was no way I was walking in five inches of snow. On a positive note, it meant I had a *lot* of snow days when I was at school so I suppose I didn't mind it that much. I'd rather be stuck indoors playing Football Manager than stuck at school doing maths.

I'm very thankful that my sister and I have always had a good relationship. We never really fought when we were growing up – even the time she projectile-vomited over me from the top bunk on holiday – and we were always really close. We still are to this day. My sister and her husband, Jonathan, have recently made me an uncle. I adore my niece and she already reminds me a lot of my sister. I just know my sister is going to make a great mother, just like my mam was with us. Needless to say, I haven't held my niece yet . . . I'm too scared I'll drop her. Try explaining that one to Social Services!

Because I'm four years older than her, I don't think my sister ever saw me as anything other than her big brother. She grew up with me being disabled so it seemed completely normal to her. If it did bother her, she certainly never let it show. Also, my sister was even shyer than I was, which made me very protective of her growing up – she always seemed so timid and quiet. Like any big brother, I felt I had a responsibility to look out for her. In reality, she was probably the one who looked after me. She knew I didn't have many mates at home so she always made sure that she played with me if she could. Of course, this usually meant I had to play with her dolls or her Wendy house, but I didn't mind.

My mam and dad seemed to cope with my disability quite well too. At least, they did to my face. I dread to think what they were going through really. It can't have been easy bringing up a disabled son but I'd like to think they've done a pretty good job. When I was little, my parents sat me down and explained to me that I couldn't talk like other people. I thought I was really special. Then I realized that every Geordie child had the exact same conversation.

Of course, they had to make sacrifices while I was growing up. My mam left her job as a nurse to look after me full time so my dad had to provide for the family. I think this suited him fine, though. He's never been a big fan of blood or hospitals and, let's face it, I had my fair share of both when I was growing up. It's almost as if he *wanted* to work. And, hopefully, not just to get away from his family . . . To be fair, Mam and Dad always shared the responsibility of looking after me. If I was busy getting ready for school, one of them would sort my breakfast out while the other tried to brush my teeth. I say 'tried' because my teeth have always been notoriously difficult to clean: my mouth clamps shut whenever anything goes near it (apart from chocolate, of course). My parents probably flipped a coin every morning to see who was going to get the shit job that day.

But, love me as they do, I think even they were glad when I moved out of home. Mainly because it meant they could do all the stuff they couldn't do while I was living with them. Such as visit restaurants with lots of stairs and cry over films about disabled children without feeling guilty.

Christmas was an interesting time in the Ridley household, and not just because we had the whole extended family around for dinner, which was always mayhem. My parents used to get me very strange and inappropriate presents. When I was ten, my dad bought me a pair of walkie-talkies, then got annoyed at me when I didn't reply to his messages. A few years later, he got me a Teddy Ruxpin bear, which used to speak and tell you a story. That was really taking the piss. This year I'm fully expecting to get a karaoke machine.

AND THE OSCAR GOES TO . . .

Of all the many gifts my parents have given me, one of the greatest was the confidence to take part in physical activities from which my disability might seem to have excluded me. With their encouragement I tried a number of different sports when I was growing up. So, come to think of it, quite possibly they thought my disability guaranteed me entry into the Paralympics as well . . . So they wanted to check whether I was good at something. Anything.

One of my earliest memories as a child, at around six years old, was my mam taking me horse-riding every weekend during the summer holidays. You probably think that was a pretty sensible choice. All I had to do was sit there and the horse would do all the hard work for me. Surely even I could manage to stay on a horse. It would be a piece of cake. As it was a horse-riding club for people with disabilities, I think Mam felt assured that I would be in good hands. It was only when we went for my first lesson that we realized things weren't going to be as simple as we'd thought.

When we got to the stables on my first day, I was introduced to the horse I would be riding. His name was Oscar and he looked beautiful, exquisite and strong. There was one slight problem: Oscar had only one eye! I'd thought this was a horse-riding club for *people* with disabilities but the horses were disabled as well. How inclusive of them.

I turned around to look at the other horses in the stable, expecting to see a horse with a missing ear, a horse with just three legs or maybe even a horse with poor mental health (invisible disabilities are real, too, even for horses). But, to my surprise, all the other kids in the group had perfectly fit and healthy horses. Oscar was the only one who was different. It's almost as if they saw the boy with cerebral palsy coming and thought I wasn't disabled enough already.

Of course, we didn't say anything. I could hardly complain about having a wonky donkey of a horse when I was pretty wonky myself. Besides, I didn't want to hurt Oscar's feelings. So, Oscar and I bonded over being doubly disabled and we became good friends for the next six weeks. In fact, we became firm favourites with each other. The partnership was doomed from the start, though. We were never going to get to the Paralympics together. I couldn't tell him where to go, and he couldn't see where he was going. All we needed was a deaf guy to be leading us around and we'd have won a round of disability bingo.

When the horse riding didn't go as planned, my parents – desperate to get me involved in some kind of sport – had another idea. You probably think it was something simple – like bowling, perhaps. No. Of course not. You obviously haven't met my parents. They decided that I might enjoy skiing. That's right. They thought it would be a good idea to take their disabled son, who struggles to walk on even the flattest, driest surfaces, up a mountain to see if he could ski. And where did they choose to take me to learn to ski? Was it the beautiful surroundings of Colorado? The breathtaking views of the French Alps? No, they chose the most miserable of all the climates: a rainy, cold Scotland in the wintertime.

I probably need to put a disclaimer in at this point. The fact is that I know my family took me skiing because they wanted us all to do something together as a family, and that's pretty adorable of them. My parents had always enjoyed skiing and I love how they wanted to involve me and my sister in that. It's almost as if they were saying, 'We're going to make sure we all enjoy ourselves *regardless*,' and that's certainly how we've lived together as a family. There was always that determination to live as normal a life as possible. I'll be eternally grateful to them for that attitude. And I really enjoyed our trips to Aviemore in Scotland – honest, Mam. It's a really pretty place and, rain, cold and grey skies aside, I have great memories of our annual holidays there.

Mainly because the complex we stayed in had some brilliant arcade machines.

I'm probably showing my age here, but my favourite arcade game was the WWF wrestling game (now known as WWE). As with most kids, I was obsessed with playing on the arcade games every day and making sure my score remained top of the leaderboard for the duration of my holiday. At one point, my name was still at the top a whole year later. Seeing my name in lights on that low-rent arcade machine in Aviemore was right up there with the greatest achievements of my childhood.

Aviemore became a real home from home for us, especially when my grandparents came up as well. We got to spend some lush family time together, going on lovely walks and having some great nights out. I'll treasure those memories for ever. But, to be honest, I could take or leave the whole skiing part of the holiday. It's not that my parents pushed me down from the top of the mountain and left me to my fate. They thought about how they could inflict misery rather harder than that and found a disabled ski club I could join. After what had happened with the disabled horse-riding club, I was wary from the start.

As no one in their right mind would trust me to go down a ski slope on my own, my parents had to put a harness on me. If this sounds inhumane, that's probably because it was. I felt like I was a husky pulling my mam behind me. And I wasn't getting minimum wage . . . or dog biscuits. But it meant I could ski down while my mam kept hold of me from behind and controlled which direction I went in. Hopefully, things have moved on since then and the equipment disabled skiers now use is a bit more advanced, but I loved being able to ski down a mountain (almost) on my own. It was a great example of how someone else's bright idea has made such a difference for me. Of course, my balance is so shit that I never got very far, harness or not. I was always falling face first into the snow . . . and it's a fact that Scottish snow is bloody freezing, much colder than any other type.

If you've ever seen a guy with cerebral palsy hurtling out of control down the Aviemore ski slopes towards impending doom, while everyone else dives out of the way, comic-strip style, you'll know that skiing was never going to be the sport for me. Now imagine seeing a whole group of us coming down together, an army of disabled skiers taking out everyone and everything in their path. I'm not sure that the founders of the disabled ski club had this carnage in mind when it was formed, and how they ever got signed off by Health and Safety I'll never know, but being part of the disabled invasion was very enjoyable every year.

Despite these childhood traumas, I haven't ended up hating every sport. I do like football, although, as I support Newcastle United, sometimes that's debatable too. My love affair with Newcastle started at primary school. My best friend at the time, Stephen Miller, was a massive fan of the Toon Army and he invited me to a game. Stephen has cerebral palsy, too, and we were in the same class together. (Incidentally, he has gone on to become a successful Paralympic athlete, but I don't hold that against him.)

Anyway, I went along with Stephen and his family to watch my first ever game of football at St James' Park and I loved it. I'm not sure why, because Newcastle were in the old second division back then, Ossie Ardiles was the manager, the team were average at best and I'm fairly sure we got beaten 2–1 on the day. And yet I went back for more. I was overawed by the atmosphere in the stadium, and the passion of the fans was incredible to witness first hand. I know a lot of people say it these days, but Newcastle really do have some of the best fans in the country, and I realized that from day one. I wanted to be part of that communal experience every week. I wanted to feel that rush of adrenalin when we scored over and over again. And I wanted to show the lads my support . . . even if I was rubbish at the football chants and not that great at clapping. Whenever I went to swear at the referee, auto-correct always called him a 'winker'. Nevertheless, I had fallen in love for the first time and Newcastle United had my heart.

TWO FOR JOY

Stephen and I were both members of the Junior Magpies Club. This was a club for the young supporters of Newcastle and we used to get together every Sunday and play football at Newcastle's training ground in Benwell. We were two of only a handful of disabled members. All of the other kids were able-bodied. Stephen was the sensible one of the two of us. He decided to be a goalkeeper. That meant he could just stay in nets for the whole game and not have to run around everywhere. To his credit, he was a very good goalkeeper. But, as you've probably guessed by now, I wasn't that sensible. I decided I wanted to be a striker. Even back then, I wanted to be the centre of attention. This is probably why Stephen is such a successful athlete now, and why I've ended up dicking around on stage for a living.

Of course, I was really good at dribbling, just not the right sort of dribbling. And I never survived a game without injuring myself. The other kids were bigger and stronger than me and, most importantly, they didn't have wobbly legs. I don't think I ever managed to kick the ball in a straight line. I always ended up with bumps and bruises or a bloody nose. And I loved every second of it. I dread to think of the stress I put my parents through each week as they watched helplessly from the sidelines. I guess I just wanted to be like every other kid, and I didn't see why I shouldn't try to compete with them. Surprisingly, I was still the first to be picked for a team every week, but I think that was because when I tripped over my own feet in the penalty area the referee was too afraid *not* to give my team a penalty.

I'm really impressed at the number of sports that have been adapted for disabled people. It's great that so many are inclusive these days, and the opportunities for disabled children are incredible. It illustrates exactly how we can open up all aspects of society so that we see the disabled represented more fully. Before long we'll be adapting versions of classic board games. There could be a very special edition of Guess Who? in which all the characters have disabilities. No one would ever win, because everyone would be too afraid to describe their character in case they caused offence. The questions would be fun. Does your person have trouble speaking properly? Is your person incontinent? Does your person have crayon around his mouth? You could also have a disabled version of Monopoly, where every space is just free parking. And, of course, there could be a disabled version of Buckaroo, where the donkey only has one fucking eye.

In adult life a lot of people ask me if I've ever competed in the Paralympics. I reckon they think it's like school sports day where everyone gets to take part, no one is allowed to lose and everyone gets a medal at the end, regardless of how unfit and talentless they are. The reality is that to compete in one of the world's greatest sporting events, you actually have to be good at sport, like my friend Stephen. Imagine that! And I'm not. At all. I can hardly walk, never mind run, so obviously I'd be shit in the Paralympics.

That's not something I should have to apologize for. Disabled people are every bit as entitled as the able-bodied to hang around at home all day being totally unfit, and one area of sporting endeavour to which I brought a Paralympian's level of dedication from a very early age was playing computer games.

Like a lot of kids, I could do this all day and not get bored. I should probably keep my obsession with Football Manager under wraps for this book and save it for *Vol. 2: My Heroic Recovery from Addiction*. But I also loved Sensible Soccer, Cannon Fodder and Theme Park. I even roped my grandad into playing them with me when no one else was around.

My nana and grandad always visited our family on a Saturday (I think that was Nana's excuse to check up on everyone), and I looked forward to seeing them. That was when I forced him to play computer games all afternoon . . . until Nana came to save him. Of course he didn't mind. My grandad was cool like that, and playing games on the computer with him is one of my favourite memories of us together. Nothing was ever too much trouble for him as long as I was happy. He was the sort of person who would do anything for anyone. He had a really big heart. Everyone called him 'Eddie', even though that wasn't his name. I'm still not sure why. But everyone who knew him loved him. I know I did.

I would often visit their house when I was young. They had several dogs and my grandad and I would take them for walks in the woods. I'll never forget those walks because it was just us two (well, not counting the dogs) enjoying spending some time together. He wasn't just a grandad but also a proper good friend I was really close to. Oh, and he gave great back scratches!

So it hit me hard when we lost him a few years ago. And that he never got to see what I've achieved in comedy is a big sadness. I hope he'd be proud of me, though, because just by spending time with me he had a big hand in making me into the person I am today.

Being as thoughtful as they are, my parents had always tried to give me the best time possible when we went on our summer holidays. I was always very close to my cousins when I was younger, so the families decided to go to Florida together one year. My lasting memory will always be of me and my cousin Scott, chasing the Teenage Mutant Hero Turtles and trying to get their autographs. Looking back at it now, it seems very strange indeed to be running around after a bunch of blokes dressed in silly costumes, but back then it was just a lot of fun.

We have already established that having cerebral palsy and running don't really mix very well. When I pick up a bit of speed, I can't stop running that easily. In fact, the only thing that stops me is a brick wall or if I trip over and fall flat on my face. God knows what the Turtles must have thought when they saw a disabled guy running like a drunk ostrich towards them at speed. And I'm not sure what was going through their minds when they realized I was travelling directly at them, like some sort of human bowling ball.

But I knew exactly what Leonardo was thinking as I bumped into him with all of my weight propelling me forward and knocking us both over. In fact, I didn't need to read his mind: he very clearly wasn't too happy about it. At that tender age, I had never heard language like it before, and especially not from one of my heroes. Eventually I got Leonardo's autograph, but I could never watch the Teenage Mutant Hero Turtles in the same way again.

My family and I took full advantage of my disability while we were at the Florida theme parks. If you've ever been to the likes of Disney World, you'll know how long and crazy the queues are, forever twisting and turning. You think you're getting near to the front of the queue and then you turn the corner and see there's still another hundred people in front of you. Well, it turns out that if you're disabled you get to jump straight to the front of the queue for all the rides. I thought this was brilliant. Finally my cerebral palsy was benefiting me. My family all enjoyed the perks as well – a whole mob of us appearing at the front of every queue, without a care in the world. The other people in the queue . . . not so much. And, to be fair, I would have been pissed off too if I'd had to watch a large bunch of people just walk up to the front – parading their disabled person like a trophy. But you have to play the disabled card when you can, so I was never that sorry. I mentioned to my dad that to cover costs he should rent me out to other families so that they could jump the queues as well. I thought it was a really smart idea, but he didn't agree with me. All these years later I still think it'd make quite a lot of money. Maybe I'll take the idea on to *Dragons' Den* and see what they have to say about it.

'Are you as clever as Stephen Hawking?'

You'd be surprised how often I get asked this question. It's mainly by taxi drivers who are trying to be funny but are in fact extremely stupid. I'm clearly not as clever as Stephen Hawking or I wouldn't be working as a comedian in Halifax on a freezing Friday night in February. I like pretending to be Hawking sometimes, though. Who doesn't? It really freaks people out if they're reading one of his books on the train and I start reading it out loud over their shoulder, as if he's putting in an appearance from beyond the grave. And it's possible that I've phoned up PC World and pretended to be Hawking, telling some poor bugger who made the mistake of picking up the phone that I'd caught a virus, and now needed some anti-virus software to fix the problem. Yes, that was both childish and silly of me . . . but my mates and I also found it very, very amusing.

My favourite Hawking impersonation was when I went to see *The Theory of Everything* at the cinema – the movie about Stephen Hawking and his life. It's a proper tear-jerker and I recommend you give it a watch if you haven't already. I might join you because I didn't go to the cinema to *watch* it. That would be too sensible.

I went so that I could sit at the back, say random sentences on my talker, and totally mess with other people's heads.

Hawking would say something on screen and I would exclaim from the back row that I didn't say that at all, and that the movie was putting words into my machine. One guy in front of me seemed to be really impressed that it was being shown in surround-sound. Then, at other times, I would type what I thought Hawking was going to say just before he said it. This was especially fun when he was talking to his wife and I kept saying, 'I don't love you.' You can probably guess that I never got to see the end of the movie that day. I was asked to leave about half an hour into the film. Some people have no sense of fun.

THE PERCY 3
HEDLEY
SCHOOL
FOR
SPASTICS

espite not being quite as clever as the professor, I like to think I did pretty well at school, but I'll admit that as a kid I sometimes struggled to make friends. Mainly because I went to a school for disabled children, which was a forty-minute taxi ride from my home, so it was hard if not impossible to build friendships beyond the school gates. Back then the educational institution I attended was called the Percy Hedley School for Spastics. They certainly knew how to make us feel good about ourselves. Thankfully, things have moved on a bit since I went to school thirty years ago, and they no longer call us spastics. Lots of other names, but not spastics.

In mainstream schools, it's the fittest and most attractive children who are the most popular, but it wasn't like that for me. At my school, you were judged on how bad your disability was. If there wasn't much wrong with you, you were bullied for being too normal. And, let me tell you, you don't want to be on the receiving end of an electric wheelchair.

Reluctant to come off second best in any game of Disability Top Trumps, I also developed epilepsy when I was a teenager. I say 'developed', like I'd been working on it in the laboratory for most of my life – a disabled mad professor. What I mean is that I had my first epileptic episode when I was fourteen. The scariest part was that it came out of nowhere. Up until that point I didn't even know I had epilepsy. Whether I'd always had it and it had been dormant until then or whether I developed it in some other way has always puzzled me. Not even the doctors could give me a definitive answer after months of prodding, poking and brain scans. It just suddenly appeared one day, as if my body had decided I wasn't disabled enough already. Thanks for that!

At the start, I wasn't having full-blown epileptic fits. Instead, my body would just go into spasm for a few seconds at a time without explanation. This would be scary for anybody. I think most of us have a pretty good idea of how we expect our bodies to behave day to day, so when something goes wrong or doesn't work as it should, it's very disconcerting. This is especially the case when you're a teenage boy and your body is already changing a lot because of puberty. When you're growing hair in every possible area for the first time, the last thing you want is for something else to come along and complicate matters further. At least I didn't have to worry about my voice breaking (that had happened when I was a baby).

The first few times that my body went into spasm it really freaked me out. I just didn't know what was happening. Thankfully, it always seemed to happen at school so I was surrounded by people who could look out for me and help me. Not that it caused much of a problem. My spasms were usually over as quickly as they began. I knew it shouldn't be happening, though, and that was what frightened me most.

Quite a few of my mates at school had the condition so I knew what it looked like when someone was taking an epileptic fit. First they would zone out, then eventually start to have convulsions. This would happen for a few minutes and then it'd stop. To be honest, it always used to scare me whenever I saw one of my friends taking a fit. I felt helpless because I knew I couldn't do anything to stop it. But, because my spasms were a lot different, I didn't even associate it with having epilepsy. I wasn't fitting or blacking out. Obviously, I know now that epileptic fits come in all different forms. You don't have to black out and roll around the floor like a break-dancer but when I was fourteen I had no idea. It was only when I went to the doctor to have it checked out that the E-word was first mentioned.

I was referred to a specialist straight away and they started to do tests on me to see what was wrong. I've had many tests in my life but these were probably some of the most daunting I've ever had – and I've sat GCSE maths. The doctors needed to have a good look at my brain activity so they gave me an EEG scan (this stands for electroencephalogram, so you can see why I've used the abbreviation). It's a non-invasive test that records electrical patterns in your brain. Sounds pretty harmless, doesn't it?

Well, it was . . . except that I had to lie on a bed and be transported into a massive scanner that surrounded my whole body (I really hope technology has moved on since then so no one else has to go through that). I'm slightly claustrophobic so I didn't enjoy the experience at all, and it happened on quite a few occasions. I just remember panicking as I went into the machine and thinking I'd get stuck in there for ever. I was also worried that they would discover I had no brain at all. Given some of my school marks at the time, that wouldn't have been entirely surprising.

After this particular torture was over, the doctors finally diagnosed me as having epilepsy and I was given medication to help control it. It was still a mystery as to why it had decided to start when I was fourteen.

My epilepsy has got worse as I've got older. What started out as mild spasms are now full-blown fits where I black out for a few minutes. I can't really remember when I had my first, but the feeling is always the same. I can sense that it's coming. I still don't know if this is a blessing or not. On the one hand, it serves as a warning to me that I'm going to collapse any second and I can usually find myself somewhere safe to sit or lie while I ride it out. But, on the other hand, I can't stop it happening, however hard I try to focus and concentrate, and that's a very frustrating position to be in. Eventually the fit will take hold of my body and I'll start convulsing. I thought this was frightening to watch as a bystander but experiencing it yourself is much worse. Not that you know what's happening until it's over and you start to come around.

Once I'm in the middle of a fit, I lose a few minutes of my life. My brain just doesn't register what's going on at all. So it's quite a weird sensation when I finally regain control and realize I have no clue as to what's happened for the last few minutes (I've had Tinder dates where I wish this blank could have happened). If I've been lucky, I'll come around and find myself on a sofa or bed but there's been a few instances when I've found myself on the floor surrounded by strangers because I haven't been able to get myself to a safe place in time. This is horrible. What makes it worse is that I'm still pretty drowsy for ten minutes or so after coming around, and using my talker when I'm like that is virtually impossible. It's like trying to send a text message when you're really drunk.

TEGRETOLS, I'VE HAD A FEW . . .

Thankfully, I don't have episodes that often. The medication I'm on is called Tegretol (also known as carbamazepine – another tongue twister) and it controls my epilepsy really well. I haven't had any sort of fit for over three years now. Some of the side effects of Tegretol make me laugh. They include:

Loss of balance/coordination
Unsteadiness
Feeling weak
Leg cramps

I mean, come on.

However well it's controlled, I have the constant fear that I may take an epileptic fit at any moment. Although my epilepsy hasn't affected my life as much as it does those of some of my friends, it still does impact on me quite a lot. I definitely can't afford to miss taking my pills (one in the morning, one at lunchtime and two at night, in case you're interested), because that results in a chemical imbalance in my body and means I'm more likely to take a fit. Because I find it difficult to take tablets with water (swallowing isn't my strong point), I usually take them at mealtimes instead. This means I have to plan when I eat to take my medication at the right time. It also means that I can't afford to miss many mealtimes. There have been numerous times when I've come home from a gig at 2 a.m. and just wanted to jump straight into bed and sleep, but I never can because I need to eat and take my Tegretol.

I also have to watch myself when I'm exhausted because it's more liable to happen then. Otherwise it happens randomly. It's quite an annoying disability to have because you can never predict when it's going to strike next. And that last sentence may be the biggest understatement ever.

It's illegal to have a driving licence if you've had a fit in the past twelve months. This isn't too much of an issue now because I don't drive my car any more, although I do frequently still use my licence as a form of ID. It's the only thing I own with a decent photo of me on! But the driving thing was a massive deal when I was in my late teens and early twenties. My car played a big part in enabling me to be relatively independent. I could go anywhere I wanted. So when I took an epileptic fit and had to report it to the DVLA, losing my licence for at least a year, it was heartbreaking. It felt like they'd taken a bit of me as well because I no longer had that freedom to go out and do what I wanted.

When you're younger, the lifelines that keep you in touch with people living normal lives are even more important. That's why I'm so glad that during my secondary education I went to a mainstream school for some of my lessons. By then, I had moved from Percy Hedley to Barbara Priestman School in Sunderland. As a Newcastle fan, I found going to school in Sunderland very tough at times, especially when the Mackems won the derby games. Barbara Priestman had a mainstream school right next door to it, called Thornhill, and I went there for science, history and French lessons, among others. They failed me on my French oral exam, by the way. Obviously, I couldn't actually take it because of the whole not-being-able-to-speak thing, so they had no choice but to give me a fail for that part of the exam. I still find it pretty amusing.

Attending a mainstream school for some of my lessons benefited me a lot, not only educationally but also socially. For a start, it meant that I was in an environment where everyone had similar academic abilities, so I was being challenged to keep up with the rest of the group, and that's something I thrived on. I have no doubt that I got better GCSE results because of it. Of course, that won't be the case for everyone – it depends on your particular disability – and special-needs education is vital for a lot of children.

The level of support I received at Barbara Priestman was incredible and it helped mould me into the person I am today. It's a massive shame that special-needs education is now so underfunded. The closure of special-needs schools because local authorities can't afford to run them is a very worrying trend. By forcing disabled children into mainstream education (or maybe no education at all, because they can't cope and eventually drop out of the system), they are setting them up to fail in life before they've even got started.

Of course, every child is different and that is why there can be no hard and fast rule when it comes to educating disabled kids. Some might benefit from going to mainstream school and that's great. But many are going to struggle in that environment. They won't get the attention they would have in special-needs education, the attention they may need to flourish in life. They'll be put in a class with thirty other kids and expected to excel regardless.

Mainstream schools are mostly motivated by exam results and their Ofsted score because that's what the system demands, so they're certainly not going to care that much if one or two children aren't coping. They'll just be put in a lower-ability class and forgotten about. And then there's the other stuff, such as physio and health, that many mainstream schools aren't equipped to deal with. Why should someone miss out on vital physio sessions, which could help improve their lives for years to come, just because the school they've been sent to can't provide them?

I appreciate that I'm talking quite generally here and that there will be some mainstream schools that are great with their disabled students. But, at the same time, there are many schools that aren't, and the range of issues that disabled children face is just too broad for one policy to serve all their needs. Disabled people deserve a good education system just like everyone else; they don't deserve to be left behind and forgotten about. Mainstream schools and special-needs schools should co-exist, so that the choice of what is suitable for a particular individual is left with the child and their parents. I was lucky enough to benefit from having the best of both worlds, and I haven't turned out too badly.

Thornhill was probably the first time I really socialized with people of my own age who didn't have a disability. That was a real eye-opener for me, and for them. I'm sure I was one of the first disabled people some of them had met, and their contact with me was certainly the first time they had interacted with a disabled bloke on a regular basis. Initially they didn't know what to make of me, and I didn't know what to make of them. It took a while for us all to get comfortable around each other. But once I relaxed a bit and started to make them laugh by being the funny one of the group, it soon became a lot easier for me. Well, as easy as it can be when you're a Newcastle United fan going to a school in Sunderland.

I made a lot of friends at Thornhill and it was brilliant to feel accepted by my new peer group. It showed me there was a whole world out there that didn't revolve around a disability. I think I endeared myself to my new mates by letting them use my disability to their advantage as well as mine. We used to tell the teachers we needed to leave class five minutes early so that we could beat the rush when all the other pupils were let out. We also told them I couldn't walk to my next lesson on my own and that I needed someone to walk with me as my chaperone. None of this was true. We just wanted to get out of science early. The teachers were too afraid to question it so they allowed it to happen.

By the end of the school year, we were finishing lessons at least ten minutes before the rest of the class (five minutes to pack my bag and get my coat on, if I really exaggerated my struggle with it, and five minutes to meander to my next lesson). Not that any of my mates actually walked me to where I needed to be next (I was perfectly capable of getting myself there). Once we were out of sight of the teacher they would run off and have a quick cigarette instead. If karma really does exist, they probably have smoking-related health issues now and my fantastic teachers are retired on a fat pension.

Going to schools quite a long way from home made socializing outside school hard. When your best friend lives more than an hour away, it's difficult to arrange to meet them at weekends (especially as this was in the age before mobile phones and social media, and I'm not the most mobile person). So, although I had some great friends at school, I was quite a loner when I was at home. 'Loner' is a difficult word, isn't it? It's always the loner who turns out to be the psychopath. Spending time alone didn't quite tip me over that edge but it did turn me into a computer geek. It meant my best friend during the summer holidays was my Amiga 500.

I did get to see my friends from school sometimes: our parents would drive us to each other's houses so we could hang out together. Back in the day we called it 'playing'. Stephen and I especially spent quite a lot of time at each other's places. I remember playing Sensible Soccer with him on warm summer days. Both of us were shit at it because neither of us could control a joystick with much accuracy. I'd concede, he'd concede, and on it would go, so our matches always ended up being 10–10 draws. Huge score lines revealing deep ineptitude. It was a bit like watching Newcastle under Kevin Keegan.

When we managed to get together, my mates and I got up to our fair share of mischief, like most kids. But we had better pranks. Our school was located next to a church, so one day I decided to borrow my friend's wheelchair, propel myself to the church doors, and wait for the congregation to come out. I already knew that at least a few people would pat me on the head, like I was a pet dog, and say, 'Bless you.' It's something every disabled person has to put up with at some point in their life. Anyway, I was right – I should have put a bet on – and almost straight away an old lady thought it was perfectly acceptable to pat me. Only this time I didn't look away and cringe. I didn't give her one of my dirty looks that says, 'What the fuck do you think you're doing?' This time, as soon as her hand touched my head, I stood up. It was a miracle. I was healed! And she was surprised. Maybe a bit pissed off.

WHO NEEDS ENEMIES?

During my time at Percy Hedley, I was a member of their Cub Scout group. On a trip to Edinburgh Zoo, a friend (who had only one arm) and I decided to freak out the other kids in the pack. We went into the lion enclosure and, playing to the crowd, I asked him to point out which of the lions had taken his other arm. We thought we were hilarious but the Cub Scout leader didn't share that opinion at all. The journey home was very long and awkward.

My favourite bit of mischief was when a blind kid and I were playing tricks on each other. It wasn't anything nasty, just the normal sort of thing that teenagers do to make the school day more bearable. He would turn up my talker to maximum volume on the sly, so I gave myself a fright when I spoke. And then

I would retaliate by changing his plate around at lunchtime, so he ended up eating someone else's food. This escalated throughout the school year until one day he decided it would be fun to hide my talker. Not just for a few minutes, but for most of the day. The teachers were going crazy at me for losing such an expensive bit of kit, and not being able to speak was sending me crazy too. Eventually the teachers found it hidden behind one of the boys' toilets. No one ever worked out how it had got there, but the smile on my blind mate's face said it all.

I had to get my revenge and it had to be good. A sneaky look at the register meant it was easy to find out his address, and I guess that even back then my writing skills were pretty good, so I wrote him a really erotic letter from a pretend girlfriend. My turn to grin as I put the letter in the postbox the next day, because I knew for a fact that his mam would have to read every filthy last word to him.

I will admit that having only a few friends at home in Medomsley was hard to cope with at times. Obviously I had my sister and grandad to play with, and my parents tried to get me to see my classmates as much as they could. They even brought some of my friends on family holidays so that I would enjoy them more. But, in the end, there was only so much they could do to create a social life for me.

That's probably why I'm socially awkward today. Despite having a job where I have to perform on stage most nights, I'm an incredibly shy person until I get to know someone. Part of that is obviously because of my disability and worrying about what people are thinking of me, but part of it is because I've always been comfortable in my own company, so I find striking up a conversation with a stranger a bit difficult. I'm a right

Mr Chatterbox when I get going and I love talking to people. It's just those awkward first few moments that I find hard.

My social unease has definitely got better over the years. Going to New College Durham to do my A levels was when I really started to come out of my shell. Even then, I kept myself to myself for the first year. I went to college, sat through my lessons and went home again. I knew the students had a common room, and I was dying to make some new friends, but I just didn't have the balls to go in. I think I was afraid of rejection. It was only in my second year that I finally took the plunge and opened the door to that common room. And do you know what? Everything was fine! I'd been worrying about nothing, as I often do.

I went in and sat down, and met at least five people in my first hour. Needless to say, I enjoyed my second year much more than my first, because I had mates to share the experience with. Also, because the college was closer to home than my school, it meant that I got to see those friends in the evenings and at weekends as well. I still remember my mates from college fondly because they were the ones who made me break out of my comfort zone.

One of the reasons why I love writing so much was because I had a great English teacher at school. How often is that the case? His name was Mr Pod and, luckily for me, he spotted my potential even before I knew I had any. I first met Pod (as he liked to be called) when I started at Barbara Priestman School, aged twelve. Funnily enough, he'd known my dad years earlier, so I think a bond existed between us from the start. He was a great teacher who seemed to have a knack of getting the best out of most people he taught, even the kids who didn't want to be there. Pod saw that I had the ability to do whatever I wanted to do: I just had to put my mind to it. He took it on himself to make sure that I did. His faith in me went a long way and it still helps today. When I aced my A levels, Pod sent me an email to congratulate me. I printed it out and it's still up on my wall almost twenty years later. It says:

I am totally and absolutely gobsmacked! What a fantastic achievement! Never mind Preston, how about Oxford? Christopher Columbus, the boy did brill. You should be really proud of yourself, I certainly am! The fact that I'm not very coherent tells you how lost I am for words to do justice to your success. The word 'congratulations' just doesn't do justice to the occasion.

Now that you've shown you can reach for the stars, don't stop there, try even higher! You never know, I might even get to make a guest appearance on This Is Your Life!

Go for it, you can do it, I believe in you!

Pod

Brings a tear, right?

My form tutor, Mrs Fraser, was another person who always looked out for me. Between the two of them, they always pushed me to do the best I could. If my essay wasn't good enough, they would tell me so. If they thought I was messing around too much in class, they would say so. No special dispensation because of my disability. No polite patronizing from either of them. Of course, I hated them for it at the time because I couldn't see the bigger picture. What teenager can? But they could. It's only now that I can look back and see what a big influence they had on me. It's amazing to have someone like that believing in you and helping you to achieve your goals, particularly when the odds are stacked against you. I'll be eternally grateful to them both.

I have always felt guilty about something, though, so I have a confession to make.

Mrs Fraser was also my art teacher and I was really bad at that. I couldn't even draw a stick man without making him look as disabled as I am. I just don't have the control. So, whenever I had to draw something for my homework, I always used to get my mam to draw it for me. Then I would trace over it and take it into class, passing it off as my own masterpiece. I think Mrs Fraser always knew that it wasn't my work, but just in case she thought she'd somehow brought out the artist in me, sorry, Miss.

'Are you drunk?'

I experienced a great sense of new-found freedom when I finally started to get out and about in the evenings, but there was one problem when I went out clubbing with my mates. On a night out, people always assumed that I must be drunk because I couldn't walk very well. As I've said, I do struggle to walk in a straight line and I look very wobbly even when I'm stone-cold sober, so it was an easy mistake to make. But I actually walk this badly all the time. I've been refused entry to quite a few bars and clubs because the bouncers thought I was too pissed.

One particular instance of being refused entry to a nightclub in Preston called Tokyo Jo's sticks in my mind. I had agreed to meet my friends inside. But when I got to the front of the queue, the doorman wouldn't let me in. He claimed I was 'too arseholed'. Of course I tried to argue my case but it certainly didn't help that I couldn't talk either. You try telling a bouncer you're not drunk when you can't form a sentence and you keep dribbling on their shoulder.

Eventually, I did make him realize the error of his ways and he finally figured out that I was just disabled, and not an absolute piss-head. He seemed

very embarrassed when it dawned on him and he
waved me in straight away. I couldn't resist one last
dig, though. As I walked past him and into the club, I
typed: 'You'll know when I'm really drunk because
I'll have sick all over my shoes, I'll be trying to chat up
a self-service checkout, and I'll be walking in a straight
line . . .'

I never had any trouble getting into Tokyo Jo's again.

THE UNIVERSITY OF TRANCE

4

It was when I went to university that my life really stepped up a gear. Deciding to do a degree was one of the biggest – and best – decisions I have ever made. It certainly wasn't an easy choice, but we made it as a family. I think I'd always just assumed I'd be going because that was what most people I knew were doing. For me, it was the logical next step after leaving sixth-form college. I don't think my parents were expecting that to be the case, though, so when I first mentioned it they were initially quite wary about the idea. Until then, I'd always lived at home with my mam, dad, sister and the various gorgeous dogs we owned over the years. This meant that I had always had their support in everything I did. I'd never cooked for myself, I'd never washed my own clothes – which is true of most teenagers, to be fair – but I hadn't even dressed myself. Picture that. There were huge question marks about how I would cope on my own.

I was young, naive and had been wrapped in cotton wool for most of my life. Understandably, my family was reluctant to let me go. But they also realized their little boy wasn't so little any more, and that it was time. I had reservations too. Would I starve to death in my first week? Who would brush my teeth? These are not questions that most teenagers heading off to university are asking.

Going to college had made me a bit more independent. I'd passed my driving test and had my own car. Leaving home was a whole different ball game. It was a challenge but something I felt I had to do. I knew that if I didn't do it at that point, I might never do it. I didn't like the thought of staying at home all my life and eventually becoming a burden to everyone as my parents got older. This was my chance to prove that I could be independent and I had to take it.

One decision that wasn't hard, however, was what I would study. Without a doubt, it was going to be journalism. I had loved writing ever since I was twelve or thirteen, and I used to write short stories in my spare time. I can't recall what they were about and they were probably pretty shit, but I used to love losing myself in my own little world. I still do. One of the unlikely bonuses of not having many friends when I was growing up was that I had to make use of my imagination, and I got really good at that. I used to have WWE wrestling figures when I was a boy and I would make up really in-depth story-lines about all of the characters. I think that imagination of mine has helped me ever since. It introduced me to my love of writing and, even today, it helps me when I'm writing my comedy. I'm a storyteller. Spoiler alert: not all my jokes are based on fact. I do sometimes make things up.

The first portal for things I'd written to be seen and read by members of the public was actually basketball. During my teenage years, when I first became a fan of basketball, using that leisure interest as a stepping stone to some kind of writing career was the last thing on my mind – it just seemed like another sport I was wildly unsuited to.

I didn't fall for one of the big NBA teams. I kept it local and started to support Newcastle Eagles. Admittedly I began going to games partly because I fancied one of the girls I went with, but while I eventually got over that particular crush, my love affair with the Eagles lived on and continues. Of course, if I was expecting this relationship to be any less heartbreaking than the one I was also having with Newcastle United, I was in for some major disappointment. This is the constant agony of many a sports fan, but it seems that whoever I support likes to fool me into thinking that maybe, just maybe, this could be the year they finally win something . . . and then they fall at the last hurdle. It happened quite a lot at St James' Park, and it would happen with the Eagles as well. In fact, looking back at it now, I never saw either team lift any silverware when I was there to support them in person. To rub salt into the wound, the year I stopped going to Eagles games was the year they started to win stuff. Newcastle Eagles are now one of the most successful franchises in British basketball history, and I've missed all the good times!

For a few important years in my adolescence, the Eagles were like a family to me. The players, the staff, the fans, we were all in it together, and it was great meeting up with everyone at games, both home and away. In an era when most sports stars are inaccessible and hidden away, the Eagles players were more than happy to mingle with their fans before and after games. I'm still good friends with many former players and staff now, which tells you a lot about the bonds that were forged on the edges of that basketball court.

Being the geek I was, and having already decided that journalism was what I wanted to study at university, I set up a website dedicated to the Newcastle Eagles basketball club and ran it as a hobby. Eventually, this led the team to let me run their official website. Soon I was reporting on games and interviewing players for a British basketball website called Britball. Other people were reading articles about basketball that I had written. At the time that was a very big deal to me. It was the start of my journey into journalism, which would be the bedrock of everything I would go on to achieve.

I've come a long way since reporting on yet another Newcastle Eagles defeat for Britball, but the experience I gained from doing that has remained with me ever since. Good writing is the key to success in both journalism and comedy, and I'd like to think that my time working with the Eagles was where I learned the basics of my craft. So, it didn't matter if I wasn't sporty, and it didn't matter that I'd never make it to the Paralympics, because I had my heart set on another career, one that involved lots of words and the use of my brain rather than my body.

UCLAN HO

My family was very supportive of my decision to go to university. They've always got behind me. Of course, they've had a massive impact on my life and I wouldn't have been able to do nearly as much as I have without them. I'm lucky that I have such a close family who are always willing to lend a hand when I need it. Maybe that's why I felt so confident that I could cope at university, because I knew they'd always have my back if anything went wrong.

My parents and I started looking at the various universities which did courses in journalism. There was one in London but that was too far from home for a mammy's boy. Some kids want to get as far away as possible, but not me. We also went to visit the university in Liverpool. It had a good reputation for its journalism course but the campus was spread out across the city and we weren't sure I'd be able to manage in such a big place . . . and after being there for just a day I was sick of everyone reminding me that the Beatles came from there. Did you know? Yes, me too.

It was a similar story when I visited Edinburgh University. It quickly became obvious that I'd never cope with all the cobbles and hills. What I didn't know then, of course, was that I would end up having to go there every August for the Edinburgh Fringe, and the cobbles would still be unmanageable.

Eventually, we decided on the University of Central Lancashire (UCLan) in Preston. Their journalism course came highly recommended, it wasn't too far from home, the campus was fairly compact and, most importantly, Preston was much flatter than Edinburgh. We just got a good vibe from the place when we visited. The support they gave their disabled students was second to none. My family and I had no idea where to start with things like organizing note-takers for my lectures, or getting accessible accommodation, or anything else to do with the logistics of my independent living, for that matter. I was the first person in the family to go to university, so this was a whole new world for all of us.

UCLan made the transition from relying on my parents at home to living independently at university almost seamless, and I have huge respect for the people who made that possible. They sorted it all. I was to have a carer come in twice a day for an hour each time. But, amazingly, the rest of the time I was going to be on my own in the big wide world. I couldn't wait!

You're probably thinking that choosing journalism as a career is a bit silly for someone who can't communicate very well. After all, most of a journalist's time is spent on the phone or at press conferences, *talking* to people, making connections, trying to get the big story. And, yes, maybe it was a bit ambitious of me to want to become a journalist. But, let's face it, being a stand-up comedian when you can't speak is equally crazy. I guess I just like making things hard for myself. I knew that getting a job in journalism would be harder because of my cerebral palsy. I just didn't see that as a reason not to try. I had my heart set on it. I was always going to be a journalist. I was always going to go to university. And I was always going to be independent. My disability is a big part of me, but I've never let it rule my life. Some people would say that's brave or courageous, but I don't believe it is. And I hate being called that. There are plenty of people who deserve to be called brave. I'm just a guy trying to get on with his life.

Initially, it was tough. The first few days especially. My parents came down to drop me off at university and they stayed in a nearby Holiday Inn for the weekend to make sure I settled in all right. And I was coping pretty well. Until they had to leave to go back home to Medomsley. As soon as I'd waved them off and closed the door to my room, I started to cry. I'd never spent that much time away from my family before – I'd been on school trips a few times but even then I'd got homesick pretty quickly. So, the realization that I was all alone, hundreds of miles from home, living with strangers, and that this would be my life now, hit me hard.

It's a tough time for lots of students, but I was coming at it from a different place altogether. My parents really had done everything for me until then. This was also before mobile phones were really common and dial-up internet was still a thing. I had never felt so far from home in my life. I curled up into a ball on my bed and cried, wishing my mam was there to make it all better again.

It took me a while to pull myself together, but I knew I had to. My room at university wasn't going to decorate itself. Once my *South Park* and *X-Files* posters were up, my VHS videos were arranged by genre on the shelf (God, I really am old, aren't I?), and my laptop was set up to play Championship Manager, I started to feel a bit more at home. What a bachelor pad I'd created. I was irresistible, surely.

The hardest part was still to come, though. There were five rooms in Flat 11, Ribble Hall, and I had seen other people coming in and out all day, moving their stuff in. But I was yet to meet any of them properly. Being as self-conscious as I am, the prospect of meeting my new flatmates was daunting. What if they didn't like me? What if they didn't understand about my disability? What if they were complete dickheads? The five of us had to share a communal kitchen so I was trying to feed myself when I first met the four other lads I'd spend the next year living with. The fact we're still good mates now probably tells you all you need to know about how the introductions went. As usual, I was worrying about nothing and we all got on fine . . . except that I was *much* tidier than anyone else in the kitchen, but I'm totally over that now. I barely think about having to live in that squalor any more. I certainly don't hold any grudges.

Simon, Stuart, Nick, Gavin and I hit it off straight away and decided to go out for a drink to celebrate our first night living together. During our first night out as a gang, we met some girls from the flat above us too – Michelle, Donna 1, Nic, and Donna 2. I've been called some rude names in my time, but Donna 2 is right up there. I made a lot of good friends during my time in Preston but none quite like those I met on my first night. These friendships have survived the test of time (apart from Gavin, who seems to have disappeared: he's probably still in the library). It's hard to describe what their friendship meant to me, but they made a very shy bloke from Newcastle, who was feeling a bit lonely and vulnerable, very welcome.

Putting my disability to one side for a moment, I was a boy from a quiet village in the North East – the sort of place where everyone knows everyone else, the sort of place where everyone says hello. And the sort of place where my grandma would eventually find out if I had been naughty or not. Suddenly I was among all these different people, going out every night, having fun and enjoying being young. It was my first taste of independence and I loved every second of it. So much so that I didn't really want to go back home when term was over. My friends, my life, my independence were all in Preston and I wanted it to last for ever.

All that said, living independently for the first time in my life was a massive step forward for me and I felt out of my depth for quite some time. Even now, I still wonder if I'm grown up enough to live independently. I can't even put my socks on without causing myself a bad head injury. I was so used to being looked after by my mam and dad that I didn't know what to do at all. My first big weekly shop on my own was a nightmare. I wasn't sure what my mam used to buy so I just ended up buying a load of cakes, chocolate buttons, crisps, and other things not beginning with C. I had an *amazing* few days eating it all, but I totally forgot to buy any of the essential stuff. You can't wipe your bum with a delicious pizza.

It was hard to adapt to not having my parents on hand to help me when I needed it. For the most part, I had carers and support workers to help me with stuff like cooking, cleaning and getting dressed. But this also meant I had to learn to become more organized. I needed to know what I wanted for lunch so that it could be prepared for me in the morning. I needed to know what clean clothes I had left to last the rest of the week. And, if I was going out, I needed my carer to help get me ready. This usually meant getting ready to go out at tea-time even though I wasn't going out until much later. So there I'd be in the late afternoon, hanging around in my glad rags . . .

Because I was relying on other people, I had to make sure I simplified my life as much as possible when they weren't around. In my first semester, I went commando to several lectures because I'd run out of clean pants and had no one to do the washing for me. I suspect I'm not the first student or the last to do that, though. And what's their excuse?

Going to university made me grow up in so many different ways and it was the final bit of proof that I needed to reassure myself that my disability wasn't going to stop me doing anything that I wanted. Until that point I'd really wanted this to be true, but I just didn't know for sure. There was always an element of doubt. Now I knew what I was capable of. It was liberating.

I worked hard at university, but I also played hard. That's one of my favourite clichés because it was just so true. I loved going out with my new friends. In fact, I was out nearly every night. I just couldn't get enough of my new-found freedom. Tokyo Jo's was the place every student went on a Wednesday night. It was your typical cheesy nightclub. It had a shit name, sticky carpets and played everything from Steps to Oasis. Looking back now, it wasn't brilliant – it was distinctly average at best. But when you're a young student surrounded by all your mates going crazy to 'Song 2' by Blur, a club like that seems the best place in the world.

FOUNDATION COURSE

What began with dancing to cheesy music on a Wednesday night eventually turned into an obsession with dance music – trance in particular. My discovery of dance music opened my eyes to a whole new world I hadn't known existed.

It was the mainstream stuff that first piqued my interest. Listening to the likes of Judge Jules and Pete Tong on BBC Radio 1 on a Saturday night was like taking a break from everyday life and spending time in a parallel universe, where the beats were the only thing that mattered. Never before had music had this effect on me. I'd always enjoyed good music, but I was an indie kid at heart, singing along (only in my head, of course) to the likes of Ash, Manic Street Preachers, Cast – basically all the bands you'd find on those old Shine compilation albums.

But the first time I heard dance music on the radio, I knew I wanted to hear more. So I made it my mission. I wanted to explore this new genre of music and immerse myself in it. This voyage of discovery eventually led me to a message board on the internet. A message board for people who also loved dance music and, best of all, they all regularly attended a trance night in Newcastle called Promise, at a nightclub called Foundation. I'd heard live broadcasts from other trance events on the radio and online, so I was desperate to experience a trance night in person.

I spoke to people on that message board for about a year before I found the nerve to go to a night at Foundation. And when I finally got there, I felt as though I knew most of them already. So much so that on my first visit to a Promise night I went by myself. I'd come a long way since crying in my room at university because my mam and dad weren't there.

It's very hard to describe the feeling of opening those double doors and getting hit by a blast of a trance bassline at full volume, while everyone on the dance-floor is going absolutely mental. It's really something you have to experience yourself. Trance music may not be everyone's cup of tea, but for me it was as if I'd found the release from the real world I hadn't even realized I needed. And all the people I was lucky enough to meet in Foundation felt exactly the same. They welcomed me with open arms and I made some friends for life in that club.

Being disabled, I think the dance-music scene spoke to me even more than it did other people. Dance clubs weren't just places you went to hang out and enjoy yourself: they had a much deeper purpose than that. The way I saw it, these clubs were places where people on the margins of society could find a space to escape, dance and feel free. A place where anything went and it was possible to lose your inhibitions without fear of being singled out. As someone who's never been totally comfortable in my own body, finding a place like that was awesome. I certainly wasn't the best dancer in the world but it really didn't matter how you danced as long as you were having fun. I felt that I finally belonged somewhere and it was great. Whoever you were and wherever you came from, when we were on that dance-floor the only thing that mattered was the music, and that was fine with me.

And because trance music only appealed to a certain type of person, it really did feel like I belonged to a special club. I'd already belonged to lots of special clubs, of course, but this one was better. I would see the same faces week after week and we would all look out for each other. We developed a special bond, and for someone who had grown up in relative isolation, this meant a great deal.

After my first few visits to the club, Promise became a weekly pilgrimage for me whenever I was home from university. Every Friday I would look forward to another dose of trance and dancing until the last tune at 4 a.m.

By this time I had my driving licence and my own car so I didn't even have to rely on the Taxi of Mam and Dad to get me home. At this point, you're probably thinking, How the hell did the wobbly bloke get a driving licence? Right? Don't worry, I didn't forge it. I actually passed my test when I was eighteen.

Admittedly, it was much tougher for me to learn to drive. For a start I could only drive an automatic. My car had to have special adaptations as well. And I'm not talking about alloy wheels and sub-woofers. I was definitely not a boy racer (despite my first car being a blue Vauxhall Corsa). I didn't even have any furry dice. My adaptations actually helped me to drive. For example, a knob – and I'm not talking about myself – on the steering wheel to help me control my steering better and an extension so that I could use the indicator with my right hand instead of my left. It's amazing how much a little bit of plastic can help someone's independence.

Even with all of these things, it still took me well over a year to pass my test (at the second attempt). Not particularly because I was a bad driver, but because it was another massive learning curve for me. I couldn't walk in a straight line and now I had to be able to drive in one. I was never the best driver but I was decent, and the best thing for all concerned was that I couldn't shout at other drivers. One less voice to add to the road rage. I found that flipping the finger was always so much more effective.

Looking back now, maybe me driving a car wasn't the most sensible of ideas, considering that I get tired pretty quickly and I was often doing it after dancing all night. I didn't see it like that at the time, though.

I loved having my car because it was another step to having independence. I was always driving over to see people, and I was the official taxi driver for my mates while we were at college. Without the casual racism, obviously. Perhaps inevitably,

I ended up crashing my pride and joy and it wasn't just a little bump either. I ploughed into a lamppost on the way home from Promise one night and wrote my car off. The lamppost had to be removed a few days later so at least I had the consolation of knowing I'd done a good job on it. Amazingly, I escaped that incident without even a scratch. I got another car after that but the confidence I'd had behind the wheel before the crash never came back and I ended up driving less and less. I don't drive now. Instead I have to put up with annoying taxi drivers asking if I'm as clever as that Stephen Hawking bloke.

Thankfully, some of my other mates had also learned to drive by then so it wasn't long before I was travelling further afield. One of my most memorable clubbing experiences was when I went to the Creamfields festival near Liverpool, which takes place every summer. This was my first time going to a music festival, a rite of passage for anyone. I'd be travelling down in a bus full of my mates, so I was very excited about the whole thing. I couldn't wait to dance to trance in a field on a sunny summer night surrounded by all my friends and ten thousand strangers. It was escapism at its very best. But first I had to convince my parents to let me go.

Even though I was about twenty-one, my mam and dad were still very protective of me, and that has always been the case. Even now, they're very good at looking out for me and I suspect they always will be. It's understandable: I'm their son, and any parent wants to be sure that their child is safe. The fact that I'm disabled makes me more vulnerable in their eyes. Finding the right balance between making sure I'm okay and making sure I can live as normal a life as possible is a real challenge, and it's to their enormous credit that they've always managed to juggle those two things so well.

I've never felt that they stopped me doing anything I wanted to do. They've just made sure that I've never done anything too stupid. I respect them a great deal for that. Teenagers and young adults are not always the best judges of what's good for them. With Mam and Dad's guidance, I've learned how to look after myself so much better as I've got older. So, while I might not have appreciated having protective parents when I was growing up, I can now see that they had my best interests at heart. I'll take the voodoo doll of Dad out of the drawer and put Mam's name back into my will . . .

You can imagine their reaction when I first mentioned that I wanted to go to Creamfields. They just about coped with me staying out all night clubbing and worked hard at not worrying themselves half to death. But now I was asking to go to a festival that went on for two days and was more than a hundred and fifty miles away. Needless to say they were not impressed.

I can still hear them.

'You'll never cope, Lee.'

'You'll get too tired, Lee.'

'We'll never see you again, Lee.'

I can be very persuasive when I want to be. So I put on my best smile, took advantage of my big blue eyes and talked them into letting me go. I promised I'd be careful and that I trusted my mates to look after me. This was a lie. I didn't trust them to look after me at all. Not because they weren't good friends (they were the best), but because I knew most of them couldn't even look after themselves. If you've ever been the 'designated driver' on a night out, you'll know how loud and annoying your drunk mates can get. I'm forever being told how much I'm loved by my pissed-up friends or having to order their kebabs on the way home because they're slurring their words too much.

There's irony in there somewhere. What I'm trying to say is that drunk mates are useless, so I knew I couldn't rely on them at Creamfields. Obviously, I didn't tell my parents this. In answer to the 'Are you stupid?' question, the answer is no. As far as they were concerned, all my friends were as sensible as I was. And me telling that little white lie is probably why I was allowed to go so far out of my parents' sight.

On the bus journey down from Newcastle to Liverpool everyone was in good spirits. The music was blasting and the anticipation was building the closer we got. I could just tell that it was going to be a great day. The feeling of standing in a field dancing to music surrounded by all your mates is a feeling I love – second only to standing on a stage surrounded by people laughing at my jokes. Everyone was having the time of their lives. I was coping. I wasn't tired. I wasn't lost. I wasn't struggling at all, in fact. I was just high on life and enjoying every second.

It was when we were walking through the main tent at the festival that I realized something was wrong. The tent was packed with about ten thousand people, which made getting anywhere fast rather difficult. We were constantly bumping into other people and tripping over those who were sitting on the floor having a rest. Obviously, when you have a disability, this makes the situation harder still. So, that was stressful. But something else was wrong too. I just couldn't put my finger on it. I could see all of my friends, so I hadn't lost anyone. I was standing upright, so I definitely wasn't hurt. It was only when my mate started to talk to me that I understood exactly what was up. I went to type out my reply and it dawned on me . . . My talker was nowhere to be seen.

Now, you'd think that after carrying my talker in my right hand every day for most of my life, I would know straight away when I'm not carrying it. And I'd have to agree with you: I should have noticed that it had gone. But I hadn't and it had vanished. Cue major panic on my part. Where the fuck was my talker?

My first problem was actually explaining to someone else what had happened. After all, I was without any method of communication. But I think the fear in my eyes spoke a thousand words. It was my mate Nass who figured out what was up, which was impressive because he was a little the worse for wear after a full day at a festival. My very expensive communication device had disappeared in a tent of thousands of clubbers and the chances of getting it back were very, very slim. If anything was going to sober Nass up, this would do the trick.

There was no way I could see of finding a small computer among all of the mayhem that was unfolding in front of us. I don't know what I was more worried about: the fact that I'd literally lost my voice or that my parents, who want nothing more than for me to be safe, were going to kill me. I was certainly never going to be allowed to go to another festival. To say that I was devastated would be a massive understatement. And, as a man in touch with his emotions, by this point, I'll admit to you, I was kneeling on the grass at the edge of the tent, crying my eyes out. Wailing. It's always interesting to know how you're going to react under pressure. I can't say I was expecting to fall completely apart.

Nass sat me down on the grass and ordered me not to move. Then he started his search for my voice. I sat there for what felt like hours when, in reality, it was probably only ten minutes. With every passing second I lost more hope that I'd ever get it back. It had probably been trampled into the ground by a load of ravers. Maybe, before I discovered it was missing, I'd done some of the trampling myself. Just as the last bit of hope started to slip away, I saw Nass in the distance. He was walking back towards me . . . and he had something in his hand. Surely not! It was impossible! Wasn't it?

As he got closer and I wiped the tears out of my eyes so I could see properly again, I realized he was carrying my talker above his head, like a hero coming back from battle with an enemy scalp held aloft, like a trophy. Somehow he had retraced our steps through the tent and found it lying on the ground while loads of people danced around it, as if it was a handbag. He had done the fucking impossible! The relief I felt in that moment is something I've never experienced since . . . and something I hope I never will. To this day, I still don't know how Nass managed to find my talker. It blows my mind every time I think about it. But he'll always be a hero to me.

Another secret revealed. Sorry, Mam and Dad. But the moral of the story is that I should have had more faith in my drunk friends after all.

'Can you have sex?'

A lot of people think it's perfectly acceptable to ask disabled people if they can have sex. Contrary to popular belief, yes, disabled people can actually have sex. And if I've managed to convince someone to sleep with me, there's hope for the rest of the disabled population as well. I'm not sure why so many people assume that I can't have relationships. Obviously it'd be awkward if I started to talk dirty in bed. A bit of a juggling act, that. But I can assure you, the rest of my equipment works just fine. Well, I think it does. To be honest, I haven't used it in a while so things might be a bit rusty down there. And, to tell you the truth, I haven't always had the best of luck when it comes to dating.

THE NORMAN CONQUEST

5

Dating is difficult for most of us. What do you say to chat someone up? What do you wear on the first date? How long is an acceptable length of time to wait before you ask for their Wi-Fi password the morning after the night before? But from the personal experience of a bloke with a disability and no voice, I think it's fair to say that the dating game is much harder for people like me. At the time of writing, I have had only three serious relationships. And, let's be clear, it's not from a lack of trying.

None of us wants to be left on the shelf in the great big dating supermarket of life. The one where the most desirable people have already been taken, the cheapest have been used and brought back for a refund, and the rest of us just sit there, like Tesco own-brand red sauce: not as tasty and hardly ever picked up.

One of the problems I have with dating is that I find it hard to approach girls in the traditional sense. I don't have the ability to 'chat up' a woman, which is really just having an engaging and flirtatious conversation. The best I can do is 'type up' a woman, but that just sounds wrong. You type up your dissertation, you type up your will, and you type up your letter to your grandma, who still appreciates snail mail. There's nothing sexy about being typed up. And even if there was, most people tend to judge on looks alone; they've already made up their minds about the disabled guy in front of them before I've managed to say a word.

But it's definitely easier to chat someone up now than before I used a talker to communicate. Back in the bad old days when technology wasn't so advanced, I had to rely on sign language to get my message across. As you may be able to imagine, that's a pretty limited way of chatting to anyone, let alone a special someone. For a start, you're reliant on the person you're talking to also knowing sign language. That seriously reduces the odds. Or you have to have someone there with you to translate what you're saying. That seriously messes with the buzz. More often than not, for me, it was the latter because not that many people know sign language.

I can't believe that this is still the case. As someone who has used sign language and knows a lot of people who rely on it, I just find it bizarre that we're not encouraged to use it more widely. I strongly believe that sign language should be taught in schools. After all, it's probably just as useful as learning French. Note to Department of Education: no one speaks French any more.

The nerd in me needs you to know that sign language was made an official language in 2003 but is still not taught in the majority of schools. I have no doubt that our society would benefit greatly if it was more universally used and understood. It would enable a large group of people to be included in everyday life. A bond between the two groups would be created by the ability to communicate, and the mental wellbeing of the people using sign language would also improve, with fewer feeling isolated. I have other ways of getting my point across now, but I know too well how lonely it once felt not to have the means to speak to one of my mates. Most people take this for granted, but knowing sign language would benefit everyone, if only we were given a proper chance to learn it, without it costing us the earth.

AN APOLOGY TO MY SPEECH THERAPIST

Anyway, I digress. In my case, it usually fell to my mam to be the translator. And, let's face it, when you're a young lad who's just starting to find his feet in the world, you definitely don't want your mam there when you're trying to chat to girls. It's embarrassing.

Thankfully, I was only about eight at the time, so it wasn't like I was getting her to ask girls to sleep with me. But it still made things much more cringeworthy than they should have been. Nowadays, you can just 'poke' a girl on Facebook if you want to get to know her, but we didn't have social media back in the eighties. Our equivalent was pulling a girl's hair in the playground and then running away. Not that I was very good at that either.

Even when I got my first talker, I was shit at using it. It just seemed too much of a pain, partly because it was massive so I was reluctant to be seen with it. I remember having to carry around this huge suitcase of a device everywhere I went if I wanted to say anything. When I was a kid I had no desire to draw more attention to myself. My speech therapist at the time had to force me to use it and I was so mean to her because I was adamant that I wasn't going to. It was only when I started to use it in social situations that I began to see the benefits of this new technology. I know from speaking to other speech therapists as an adult (I'm very popular in speech-therapy circles, these days) that most children are reluctant to use their devices for one reason or another. If any speechies (that's the lingo) are reading this now, please don't give up hope. You'll get through to kids in the end, and they'll eventually appreciate the effort you put in.

So, my problems with chatting to the opposite sex started when I was young. Because I initially relied on sign language, I didn't really start talking to girls properly until I was older, when I became more integrated into society, and I missed out on some of the life lessons you pick up in the playground, beyond the hair-pulling; the subtleties of interaction that you learn just by spending time with people. And, of course, I'm very self-conscious. I'm always worrying what people are thinking about me because I'm a bit different. I've never fully been comfortable in my own body and I'm always the first to notice all my flaws and point them out to others. I don't really have confidence in most social situations, let alone romantic ones.

This all means that I usually rely on online dating. The ability to hide behind a screen and let other people see only certain parts of you is what the internet was invented for. On the flip-side, the problem with some online dating sites is that they're based on how people look. As I'm as ugly as Phil and Grant Mitchell put together, I'm at a disadvantage from the start. But there are bigger problems. Do you reveal you have a disability in your profile and hope that people won't be put off by it? Or do you leave out that vital piece of information, then have the trouble of deciding when to tell the new love of your life that you can't speak? I've tried it both ways with varying results. It's not that I want to lie to people: I just don't want them to judge me solely on my disability. It's a tough choice. It means the only matches I get on Tinder are with people too stupid to know their left from their right. And, let's face it, I can't go speed-dating because by the time I've typed a sentence I'd be moving on to the next person.

Most of my relationships have ended in disaster. I think I've been scared to take any of them to the next level because I've been on my own most of my life. Instead of letting anyone get close, I've pushed them away. It's been easier that way.

Of course, it hasn't all been bad. I was dating a single mother for a while. It wasn't love, to be honest, but, being very unsteady on my feet, pushing her baby in his pushchair was much cheaper than buying a walking frame.

It was only when I started at university that I began talking to girls, and by then I had a lot of catching up to do. I got my first proper girlfriend when I was about twenty-two. Before that, I had been too shy to ask them out or they weren't inter-ested when I did. It got to the point when I thought I was never going to meet anyone (a bit dramatic for a twenty-two-year-old, I admit). I just couldn't see how anyone could love me when I had so many imperfections. I began to think that maybe I should just accept what I had in life, and be happy with that. I certainly didn't have it bad, by any means. I was surrounded by my amazing family and friends, I had a good social life and I was generally happy with my lot. Surely that could be enough for me.

As much as my head would like me to believe that every-thing is a bit worse in life because I have cerebral palsy, I would never want anyone to think I'm blaming my condition for everything that's a bit tough. I'm really not having a whinge. My mind is a strange place to be at times. On the one hand, it enjoys seeing the funny side of everything that's happening to me, but on the other it likes to remind me that I'm different from everyone else. It does get to me at times. I can become depressed about it and wonder what life would be like if I wasn't disabled. We all wonder what life would be like in some-one else's shoes, but I'm not sure anyone would be rushing to step into mine.

I sometimes wish my busy mind would allow me to just live my life: why must it insist that I worry about everything? I'm a big worrier and a massive over-thinker. I would say that I over-think things on a daily basis, and I've been like that for most of my thirty-eight years. So it's pretty hard to break this mindset. And, obviously, that's going to have an effect on other parts of my life as well, such as when I'm trying to chat up girls and my mind starts whirring. Most of the time, I just don't think I'm good enough. And if I believe that, I'm fighting a losing battle before I've even stepped out of the house.

My disability is just one aspect of my complex but, I hope, compelling personality (at least, that's how I see it on my good days). How I navigate dating is as much to do with my own attitude to my situation as it is about the attitudes of everyone around me. I can work on my self-confidence and having a positive outlook on life, but as long as we have a government that treats disabled people as though we don't matter, and as long as we have a society that doesn't treat us as equals, I honestly don't think things will change much at all for people like me. Luckily, as I've said, I have very supportive family and friends and I'm quite open about my mental health. It's really important that people talk as much as possible about stuff that is bothering them. And I'd encourage anyone who feels similar to me to talk to someone about it. It really does help.

By the time I met my first proper girlfriend at twenty-two, I'd almost given up on dating altogether. To protect this lucky lady's anonymity, let's call her 'Norman'. For the first time in my life, it didn't bother me that I was disabled, because it was clear that it didn't matter to Norman either. We just liked each other for who we were. I think that most people would be drawn to someone like that.

I'd first met Norman out clubbing. We got chatting and seemed to click straight away. She told me all about herself, and I told her about being me. We sat there for hours just talking. It was classic boy meets girl, and I couldn't believe it was happening to me. I still remember it as one of the best days of my life because everything seemed so perfect for a change. The relationship just grew from there. We chatted every day and I looked forward to seeing her again the moment we went our separate ways. To say I liked her a lot is an understatement. But at that point we were just friends.

I wanted to ask her out properly but I kept bottling it whenever we were together. Given my social awkwardness, it made sense that I finally managed to ask her out over MSN Messenger. (Younger readers might have to google that, but it was like an ancient version of FaceTime . . . without the video. So really crap.) To my absolute surprise, she said yes. I remember spending the next few weeks on Cloud Nine. I had a girlfriend. Me. Lee Ridley. Finally off the market.

THE INACCESSIBLE ROOM

It was while I was dating Norman that I achieved yet another milestone in my life and went on my first holiday without my parents. This was a big deal for me, another moment when I managed to prove to myself and everyone else that I was independent enough to do something that maybe once upon a time I wouldn't have thought possible.

So my first holiday without my parents was with Norman and that was a big deal in terms of my independence. It wasn't any old holiday either. We decided to go to Ibiza, the clubbers' paradise. Given that we had met while clubbing and had the same taste in dance music, it was completely fitting that our first holiday together was on the so-called White Isle.

Once again, I'm sure my parents had reservations about me going all that way without them. I think the furthest I'd ever been with other people was London and that was only for a few nights, so this was another adventure out of all of our comfort zones. But if they were worried, they certainly didn't mention it to me. They just told me to look after myself and let me get on with it. That kind of faith in me has always given me the confidence to go out and do stuff on my own. I admit that I was a little bit afraid of going all the way to Ibiza, but I knew that Norman would take care of me, and I was really looking forward to spreading my wings.

I've visited quite a few places since, but I've never found anywhere that's quite like Ibiza. Yes, it *is* a great place to go clubbing. But the island is so much more than that. Everyone is welcome, whether you're young or old, a family or a couple of lovebirds, a raver or a sun-worshipper, able-bodied or disabled. It is brilliantly beautiful with breathtaking views, and stunning sunsets, like nowhere else on the planet. I'm so glad I got to share my first experience of Ibiza (and my first independent holiday) with Norman. It was perfect. And it got me itching to see more of the world.

Norman and I loved to explore new cities and discover new places. One of my favourite things to do when we were making a habit of staying in hotel rooms was to write Post-it notes and hide them for other guests to find. Just innocent fun like 'The Wi-Fi password summons Him', 'I never checked out' or 'You're a very deep sleeper – I enjoyed watching you'. When you're waiting for the room service to be delivered you need to pass the time somehow and this is one endeavour where my wobbly disabled handwriting is actually an asset: it makes the notes look more like messages from the other side. I sincerely hope that one day you'll check into a hotel room and find one of my notes because it'd make my day. Then maybe you could leave one for the next guest. We could all do with an unexpected laugh from time to time.

Of course, whenever we were booking a hotel, I was always asked if I wanted the accessible room. This question has always puzzled me. I mean, who the hell wants to stay in the *inaccessible* room? Surely, by their very nature, all hotel rooms are accessible. Or am I missing something? Does every hotel have a floor of inaccessible rooms for guests who like a bit more of a challenge? Do these floors have cleaners lining the corridor, waving Henry Hoovers in your face and trying to block your path? Is it like *The Crystal Maze*, with an assault course made up of random furniture thrown all over the place? Mattresses piled on top of each other, kettles full of boiling water ready to be tipped all over you, and a Corby trouser press that has finally come into its own? Is Lenny Henry standing at the end of the corridor, surveying the carnage, like the end-of-level boss on Super Mario Bros? And even if you survive all of this, I can guarantee that, no matter how many different ways you try it, the stupid key card still won't work in the door. You fall at the last hurdle.

Being on the road as a disabled comedian has taught me that many hotels need to up their accessibility game. A hotel may boast that it can give you an 'accessible' room, but in most cases it's pot luck whether it's truly accessible or not. The thing is, I need a hotel room with a walk-in shower because I can't manage to climb into baths. So, when I turn up to an accessible room and it just has a slightly lower bath, my heart sinks. Not only does it mean that I'm going to stink until I next go home and get a proper shower, it also means that the hotel in question hasn't really thought about accessibility, just paid lip service to it. The accessible room is essentially a token gesture on their part, a box-ticking exercise.

What makes matters more complicated is that, for some disabled people, a lower bath would be preferable to a walk-in shower. I know this because I've complained about it on Twitter, then had replies from other disabled people saying exactly that. As with anything in life, one size isn't going to fit all. The disabled come in all varieties.

I would encourage all hotels to offer options. When I'm feeling generous, I appreciate that perhaps they can only do so much but equally I think it's very important that our basic needs are met. Don't have either accessible rooms with lower baths or accessible rooms with walk-in showers. Mix it up a bit and have a few of each. Then the room is effectively tailored for each guest's particular needs. And I won't have to bathe myself in deodorant just to hide how smelly I am.

'Where's your carer, dear?'

Although I've learned many strategies for coping with the challenges of day-to-day life over the years, even I have to admit that there's still stuff I'll never be able to do.

I'll never be able to put on my socks. Trust me, I've tried. One day I got so frustrated with the whole ordeal that I ended up going to work in my shoes without any socks, hoping that no one would notice. It's a hipster thing – you wouldn't understand.

Neither will I ever be able to brush my teeth. And I definitely won't be shaving myself any time soon. Forget nicks you can patch up with a plaster, I'm scared I might cut my head off.

I have other people to do all that stuff for me. I have carers (or support workers, if you want to be all modern about it) who come in twice a day, morning and evening, to help me with certain things. Given that I'm so independent (and a little bit stubborn too), it's an interesting dynamic. Do I mind having to rely on other people to look after me? The truth is that I don't mind at all, and the reason for this is because – and even though this might initially seem ironic, it actually isn't – having someone there to help me has meant that I've been able to be so much more self-sufficient.

I first started to use carers when I went to university. Until then my family had looked after me. When I left home I knew I needed a support mechanism in place to help me survive in the big wide world. Quite simply, if it wasn't for all the carers I've had since I was eighteen, I wouldn't have been able to lead a normal(ish) life. Before I had my first, I wasn't keen on the idea of having a 'carer'. When I was younger I was narrow-minded and naive and thought that having a 'carer' meant you were incapable of doing stuff yourself. I was worried what other people might assume about me. It was only when I started using one to help me live independently that I started to understand the benefits. I'd been mistaken.

Not that all my carers have been brilliant. Far from it. There have been support workers who were constantly late, support workers who were obviously not interested in doing a good job, and I even had one who turned up drunk. I wish I was joking about that.

The thing about that particular carer was that he always had a night out on Thursday. On Friday morning he would turn up hung-over and stinking of booze. I got used to it: it was just what he did. On that particular Friday, he turned up very late and seemed to be even more worse for wear than usual. Nevertheless, I let him in and went to have my shower as he followed his usual routine of washing my dishes in the kitchen.

I thought everything was fine until I got out of the shower and couldn't hear him hard at work. In fact, I couldn't hear him at all. I went into my bedroom to dry myself, expecting him to come along at any minute to help dress me. I waited . . . and waited . . . and waited a bit longer. There was no sign of him. Slightly worried that something had happened to him, I wandered into the living room, only to be greeted with the sight of him curled up on the floor and snoring loudly.

I eventually managed to wake him up (obviously I took a photo of the scene first: it was too funny to resist, as well as being useful evidence). He was very apologetic when he realized what he'd done but it was too late. He'd had numerous chances and this was the last straw. He had to go.

This is a big problem with the care system in the UK. You just never know who you're going to get. It's entirely possible that carers feel the same way. They turn up and there's me. In my favour, at least I'm never drunk. I've had some amazing people look after me over the years but also some absolute nuggets. This is mainly because most care agencies don't pay their staff enough, so they don't get quality people applying for the job. You can't really blame someone for not enjoying their job if they're getting paid pennies and not being appreciated for their hard work. I've also known several good carers, who have loved to look after other people, but who have left the profession because they've been treated like rubbish by their employers. I was lucky in that I could speak up and complain when something wasn't up to standard. Unfortunately, not everyone has that opportunity, and I really worry about those vulnerable people.

Everyone deserves to be treated with dignity and respect when being looked after, but we know that isn't always the case. If someone can't speak up about it, maybe no one else will do it on their behalf, so they're stuck in an endless cycle of not getting the care they need. Many councils still commission fifteen-minute care visits, which makes the situation even worse. What are you supposed to achieve in a quarter of an hour? It takes me at least ten minutes to have a shower in the morning. Nothing to do with my disability, everything to do with really loving showers. So that would leave me with five minutes to fit everything else in. The system leaves clients feeling rushed to get everything done in time, and carers feeling guilty that they haven't done as much as they could have. Not to mention that for many people the time they spend with their carer is all the social interaction they get for the day. It's very unfair to deny them that most basic of all requirements just because budgets are tight and staff need to be everywhere at once.

YOU HAVE TO LAUGH OR ELSE YOU'D CRY

6

I know what you're thinking . . . Well, I don't – for all I know you might've just remembered that you left a frozen pizza on the bus, or that you forgot to opt out of that Amazon Prime 30-day free trial till it was too late (that's how they get you) – but I do know what I'd be thinking if I were you. What I'd be thinking is: How come Lee has got this far without really mentioning comedy?

Well, it's happening now, so I hope you're ready for it.

Some of my favourite memories are of watching the likes of Jack Dee and Lee Evans on TV as a kid and laughing my head off. The two are very different comedians. Lee is loud and energetic and Jack is laid-back and deadpan, but I like both of them because they're each bringing something very distinctive to the stage.

Lee Evans is a master of using his body language to enhance his act. When I used to watch him, it wasn't just the jokes that made me roll around the floor laughing, it was his facial expressions . . . and that he used to run around the stage at 100 mph. He was a comedy whirlwind. Years later, his style was to influence me a lot when I started my stand-up career. He made me realize that comedy isn't just about words (luckily for me), it's about having a big stage presence too. Over time I learned to use this to my advantage. I knew that I would need to use my body as much as possible on stage to make up for the stuff I couldn't do . . . such as talking. That's why I try to be as animated as I can be when I'm doing my comedy. I may not be able to move as well as Evans or dance across the stage in an instant but, subconsciously, I'm channelling a little bit of Lee Evans whenever I'm performing.

In contrast, my love of Jack Dee comes from how clever he is as a writer. When I used to watch him on the TV as a kid, I was just astounded by how smart some of his material was. As a budding writer myself, I had a huge appreciation for his skills as a wordsmith. What makes him even more impressive is the way he manages to deliver his material without ever breaking into a smile. He's as deadpan as deadpan can be, and I just couldn't – still can't – get my head around it. Unlike with Lee Evans and his gesturing, I'm afraid I haven't been able to pick up Jack's skill of keeping a straight face when delivering a killer gag. I regularly laugh at my own material. I just can't help it.

Lee Evans's and Jack Dee's styles of comedy couldn't have been more different but I think having their contrasting examples to learn from helped me to understand what comedy really was when I was growing up. I really liked the fact that it couldn't be put into a box and defined in a simple way. There seemed to be something for everyone and I enjoyed discovering all the different kinds. Some I found hilarious and some I thought were totally shit. But it was the start of my adventure into the world of comedy and, as a fourteen-year-old boy, I simply couldn't get enough of it.

I used to think that being a stand-up comedian must be the best job in the world. Imagine being able to bring so much joy to so many people just by standing up (or sometimes sitting down, if you're rewinding to the likes of Dave Allen or Ronnie Corbett) and telling jokes. I'd always enjoyed making my friends laugh at school and I was happy to play the fool. My mam and dad were a little less happy about that, especially at parents' evenings. But it gave me an amazing feeling. Let's face it, everyone loves to have a good laugh from time to time, and it felt great to be the one to provide that burst of happiness. Not only did it make other people feel good, it made me feel great too. I can only compare it to the feeling you get when you're at the top of a rollercoaster – you know something special is going to happen when you go over the peak, and when it does it's such a great rush of excitement and adrenalin you just want to do it again and again.

But stand-up comedy takes that idea of crowd-pleasing to a completely different level. These guys, my heroes, had thousands of people hanging off their every word, waiting for the next punch-line, and this fascinated me. I began to watch more and more.

I started off with straight stand-up, but soon moved on to panel shows and sitcoms. Then I began going to watch live comedy. Immersing myself in the world of laughter was a huge personal turning point. *The League of Gentlemen* in particular struck a chord with me, and I've loved it ever since. I'm still not sure if I got my dark sense of humour from the Gents, or if it was already in the genes – thanks, Mam and Dad – but that show just managed to bring it out in me. Either way, I owe the Gents a lot for developing my very twisted mind. It wasn't so much one specific show, though, as the whole landscape of TV comedy that nourished my sense of the world as something you could laugh at, and I'd be failing in my duty to my teenage self if I didn't take this opportunity to regale you with some of my most binge-watched shows.

FAVOURITE SITCOMS

Before I even knew what comedy was, I was watching it on television in one form or another. I remember lying on my bed late at night and channel-hopping to see what was going to amuse me next. Back then, the best stuff seemed to be on BBC Two and Channel 4 (we had only four channels to choose from). I grew up on a diet of sitcom after sitcom, which no doubt influenced and educated me in the ways of comedy. Everyone has to start somewhere and if it wasn't for these hilarious shows, I might not have developed such a twisted sense of humour.

1. *The League of Gentlemen.* My absolute favourite comedy show. I loved it so much that I waited in a

queue for a few hours when they did a DVD signing in Newcastle. I got a photo with them, then queued up again because I'd forgotten to ask for their autographs the first time around (a very British thing to do: no popping back to the front of the queue for me, unless it's officially sanctioned by Mickey Mouse). Oh, and I also blagged a massive *League of Gentlemen* poster off my local HMV's wall. I still have it. I'm their number-one fan.

For those of you who haven't seen it, it's a kind of sketch show but with an ongoing storyline based on – and built out of – the fictional town of Royston Vasey. Only this isn't just any old town, this is a very backwards town, the type of place where your grandma and grandad might have gone on holiday once upon a time. Each character you meet on the journey is worse than the last. It's so delightfully dark that sometimes I wonder if it was written specifically for me. Credit must go to all four of the Gents for producing such a master-piece of comedy. I could watch it over and over again and it would never get any less funny. Beyond my love of it, it's also stood the test of time pretty well.

When I look back to what it was about *The League of Gentlemen* that particularly appealed to me, I think I liked the fact that they were making jokes out of stuff that was a bit weird and left-field. I would have been a teenager when I watched it for the first time, so that was probably my introduction to the darker side of comedy. I didn't know it existed up until that point. So they opened my eyes to a whole new world.

For the first time I got the impression that anything could be joked about if handled in the right way . . . and I loved it. It probably encouraged me to push the boundaries in my own comedy (and I'm talking about before I became a stand-up, when I was just joking on with my mates). I think the Gents helped to show me that being different was definitely an advantage when it came to being funny. They helped me view my life in a completely different way. Suddenly my various quirks were something I could laugh at rather than be self-conscious about. After all, I do quite enjoy knowing that an audience isn't entirely comfortable. I think it's a very powerful position to be in.

2. *Bottom*. This is probably one of the first comedy shows I ever watched and I loved it. It was pretty rude for a fourteen-year-old boy, but it was also made great by the performances of Rik Mayall and Ade Edmondson, who suggested to me what life might be like when I finally left home and found myself some flatmates. Their mix of knob gags and slapstick humour – the chaos of it – was exactly what I needed when I was a teenager living in quite a steady way, and I made sure I never missed an episode (even though it was on well after my bedtime).

3. *Harry Enfield and Chums*. Another of my early favourites and one of the first sketch shows to come to my

attention. Harry Enfield and Kathy Burke nailed each and every character. Kevin and Perry were my particular favourites. They were the kind of teenagers I would have loved to be but never had the nerve. They were sulky, rude and self-centred, and I was the absolute opposite. I was never rude to my parents, like Kevin and Perry were, and I rarely went off in a sulk (if you don't count the time I swiped the family Monopoly board off the table because I was losing, but we all do that, don't we?). So, sometimes I liked to be transported into a world where teenagers ruled. I used to imagine doing something similar in my own home but I liked pocket money more than anarchy. And I needed someone to help me with my socks.

4. *Peep Show*. I liked *Peep Show* because it didn't mind being a little bit different from the rest. The way it uses point-of-view shots with the thoughts of the main characters, Mark and Jeremy, heard as voiceovers, really impressed me when I first started to watch it. They couldn't be more different either. Mark is the sensible one, but often has moments of impulsive and erratic behaviour (much like me, which is why I tend to sympathize with him), while Jeremy is naive, immature and often selfish, but considers himself talented and attractive. It has some of the best comedy writing I have ever seen as well. I think we all know either a Mark or a Jeremy.

5. *Father Ted*. I used to watch this religiously (no pun intended). I just loved how silly it could be. It provided

the perfect dose of laughter and light relief for a young bloke getting stressed out by football, exams and girls — in that order. The childlike, simple-minded Father Dougal amused me a lot. But it was the elderly, foul-mouthed, alcoholic Father Jack I really loved. *Father Ted* showed me how much fun you could have by bouncing completely different characters off each other. Something I came to use in my own sitcom years later.

6. *The IT Crowd*. I'm not sure if I like this because it reminds me of my geeky side or just because it's fucking funny. I can certainly see traits of myself in both coding-genius Moss and the work-shy Roy so maybe that's why I can identify with it so much. I've definitely used Roy's technique of turning stuff off and back on again whenever I have a technical issue and, like him, I'm a big fan of video games and comic books. There was also some-thing very authentic about *The IT Crowd*'s workplace setting, which rang true with my personal experience as an office employee for the council. It was repetitive, mundane work and you had to make your own fun to combat that. Also, although everyone gave the appearance of know-ing what they were doing – meetings, memos, phone calls, the stuff of office life – in reality no one had a clue what was going on.

7. *Red Dwarf*. I adored *Red Dwarf* when I was younger. I was really into sci-fi at the time so having a sitcom that was set on a spaceship was always going to be

right up my street. It was a highlight of Friday-night comedy on the BBC. Funnily enough, I tried to watch it recently and it wasn't quite as good as I remember. Of course the programme's the same so I guess my tastes have changed over the years. Maybe I grew up. I can't blame the show for that.

8. *Desmond's*. One of the few comedy shows we used to watch together as a family. *Desmond's* was the story of a Guyanese bloke who ran a barbershop in south London. I was fairly young when I first saw it and it was one of the shows I watched without understanding what comedy really was and why this particular family and this particular workplace were funny. It made me laugh and that was all that mattered. It probably encouraged me to watch more of the 'funny stuff' on TV, seeking out a variety of it whenever I could.

9. *Inside No. 9*. I know I should stop fan-boying over Reece Shearsmith and Steve Pemberton (who are also two of *The League of Gentlemen*), but I can't write a list of my favourite comedy shows without mentioning this one. Part comedy, part horror, it really needs a genre of its own. As with anything involving these two guys, the writing is out of this world and some of the storylines are very clever. One episode stands out in my mind. 'Zanzibar' is set in a London hotel where some strangely farcical goings-on are in store for a group of unwitting guests. What makes it impressive is that it's their own twist on Shakespearean comedy and the episode is written entirely in

iambic pentameter, the clever sods. I honestly have no clue how they come up with such great ideas and am saving up my own stupid question – the classic 'Where do you get your ideas from?' – for the day I finally manage to meet them (just getting a photo and an autograph doesn't really count).

10. *The Simpsons.* Technically not a sitcom, but I grew up laughing at it so that's good enough for me. This is one of those shows that introduced me to the idea of comedy as a *thing.* It was clever enough to have humour for kids and adults (as a kid, I felt very smug when I was able to get the jokes intended for the grown-ups), and it's another programme that has survived the test of time. And yet there is such a thing as overkill. If only Channel 4 would stop showing it every few hours . . .

11. *South Park.* Yes, I know this is the eleventh pro-gramme on my top-ten list but if I'm having *The Simpsons* then I'm definitely including *South Park* too. When it first aired, *South Park* looked all sweet and innocent because it was a cartoon. We already had *The Simpsons* pushing some boundaries, but the feeling was still 'Cartoons can't be that bad, right?' Think again. *South Park* is another show I adore because it's just so wrong, from Mr Hankey – the Christmas Poo – to the sexual-harassment panda to Jimmy, the disabled character who can't speak properly (if I don't find him offensive I don't see why anyone else should). Nothing is off limits for this show and that's fine by me.

An honourable mention should also go to Ross Noble. I first saw him live when I was a teenager and he just blew my mind. It wasn't only that his accent sounded at least something like the voice in my head: I was amazed at how quick-witted he could be in the moment, and at how random he could get. He'd start off on one tack, then veer off somewhere else, and always take the audience along with him on a completely unexpected and exciting journey. The crowd was loving it and I was in awe. I wanted to be like him, even though I knew that would probably never happen.

From a very early age I saw myself as different from most people, including the comedians I watched and adored on television. And I *was* different. All of them could walk freely, pacing around the stage, taking control of it. And, crucially, given the nature of the job, all of them could talk. Really quite well. And their voices were an integral part of their act – from Ross Noble's Geordie to Al Murray's shouty pub landlord. I couldn't utter a word, so I thought that was that. I would have loved to be able to make people laugh for a living. But, I reasoned, I'd have to make do with entertaining my mates down the pub.

So how did I get from resigning myself to not being able to follow my dreams to doing exactly that? Well, two things happened that made me change my mind about what I could and couldn't do with my life. The first of those two things happened in 2011, when I became friends with a bloke called Nathan Wood.

I was employed by Sunderland City Council at the time, and we ended up working on an event together. Nathan and I became close friends and we were always making each other laugh – he was that mate at work who makes work feel less like work. I'm so glad that Fate brought us together because, although I didn't know it at the time, meeting him would change my life for ever.

TURNING A NEGATIVE INTO A POSITIVE

We were at a music gig, being silly as usual, when he suggested I was funny enough to give stand-up comedy a try. More importantly, he reckoned it would work *because* of my talker, not despite it. He was looking at it as a plus, rather than a minus.

To be honest, I'd never given this any real thought before. I'd always assumed I wouldn't be able to do it because of my inability to speak – in much the same way that my career as an Olympic sprinter was on hold. I had never tried to think of a way around the problem, which was unusual for me because I was always thinking around problems just to do the things that other people do without a moment's thought. But this seemed like a step too far. So Nathan's suggestion took me by surprise. In a way, he'd called me out. Why *couldn't* I do it?

At the time, of course, I still thought he was crazy. I couldn't picture how it would work. No one had ever heard of a stand-up comedian who couldn't speak! The closest thing to it that I'd ever seen were the comedians in the old silent movies. The likes of Charlie Chaplin and Laurel and Hardy. But they relied largely on physical comedy, which wasn't exactly my forte either. I could certainly fall over a lot – not a problem – but never on purpose. So although I knew that you could make people laugh without saying a word, I couldn't quite figure out how I'd do it.

Nevertheless, Nathan had inadvertently reignited my dream to do stand-up comedy. Naturally, I did nothing about it. I still thought it was a silly idea but, somehow, the thought stayed in the back of my mind. Maybe I always knew I'd give it a shot one day. I just didn't know when. The timing had to be right.

The second piece of the puzzle fell into place a few months later when I went to see Ross Noble's show at the City Hall in Newcastle. Ross did a very funny bit about Stephen Hawking, which included an impression of the way he spoke. Some people might have found it offensive but I certainly didn't. I found it refreshing to see someone joke about being disabled as if it was normal. After all, people make jokes about (to pick two of many possibilities) Scottish and Irish characteristics all the time. Why shouldn't people joke about disability as well? And I don't care how clever Hawking was, he still had a silly voice – as I knew from personal experience.

The whole thing was hilarious and I wanted to tell Ross how much I'd enjoyed it. After the show, I was waiting for him at the stage door (yes, I'm one of *those* people who casually stalk their heroes, so let it be known that if you're ever hoping to say hello to me at a stage door I'm completely up for it), trying to type something out to say to him.

Suddenly I saw him come out of the stage door before I was quite ready. I'm not the world's fastest typist, though it's worth reiterating that everything I do say is worth waiting for. Panic set in as I wondered what I was going to say (quickly) that would do his show justice. I would have to think fast, as well as type fast, if I wanted to impress him. Ross walked right up to me and said hello. In that moment, I typed in: 'Do you want to see who can do the best Stephen Hawking impression?' and pressed the speak button. Ross roared with laughter and I felt great. Completely elated. I had made one of my comedy idols laugh out loud. Even in the moment I was completely aware that there was no better feeling.

Ross ended up recounting the tale of our meeting that night on his next tour – I discovered this after a friend who was there told me about it without knowing it was a story about me. My mate messaged me saying that Ross had this great new bit about meeting a guy who used a talker to speak with. At first I thought he was winding me up. Then I began to wonder if Ross had met another bloke with a talker. Surely there couldn't be two of us who had met him. I got so excited when I realized that the story *was* about my encounter with him. I had to wait another year to hear it myself but when he released a DVD of that particular tour I got the chance. I was beaming from ear to ear when I saw it.

I found out recently that Ross's version of the events of that night was quite different from mine. I met up with him for a podcast interview in 2018 and it was the first time we'd actually talked about the incident in detail. According to him, when he saw me standing at the stage door he started to panic because he thought he'd offended me by doing the Hawking bit. His heart was in his mouth as he walked towards me, thinking I was going to give him a bollocking. So when I pressed the speak button and made my joke, he was so relieved

I wasn't going to kick off about it that it made him laugh even harder.

It's something I'm still immensely proud of, but it also made me think about what Nathan had said to me earlier in the year. Maybe I'd be quite good at stand-up comedy . . . And maybe I could do it using my talker. If I could make such a good comedian as Ross laugh, then surely I could make other people laugh too . . . right?

'Shall I pray for you?'

When you're disabled, people tend to pity you a lot.
When people find out more about my disability, they
start to tell me how sorry they are. Everyone is so sorry
all the time. Sorry to hear I can't talk, sorry about my
walk and sorry I'm both ugly and disabled. They say
'sorry' is the hardest word, but I can safely say that it
isn't, because I can't say any of the other words in the
dictionary either. And, let's be clear, you haven't really
tried to say the hardest word until you've attempted to
type 'supercalifragilisticexpialidocious' into your iPad
without making a spelling mistake.

The whole pity thing means people often come up to
me and say that they will pray for me. I'll be honest
with you: I'm not at all sure why they do this. I presume
it's because they think my disability is a burden and I
need to be healed. Or a sin – either in this life or some
past existence as the despotic ruler of a remote jungle
kingdom – for which I'm now paying. Or maybe their
hearts go out to me because they realize I'll never
appear on *Strictly Come Dancing*.

You'd be surprised at how much this happens. I was
once on my way to a gig in Newcastle when the taxi
driver said, out of nowhere, possibly straight after a

throwaway comment about the weather or a bit of banter about the football, that he would pray for me. Perhaps more bizarrely, he then offered me a Bible to read on the journey because that's a perfectly normal thing to do . . . I wonder if all his passengers get the same treatment.

I had no idea how to respond, but I had so many questions going around in my head. Why the hell was he carrying around a load of Bibles in his car? Had he just burgled a Premier Inn and ransacked all their rooms? Was this a new tactic by the Jehovah's Witnesses to try to drum up some business? Whenever they used to come to my parents' house when I was younger, my parents would always send me to answer the door. Instead of asking if I believed in the healing powers of the Lord, they'd take one look at me and never come back. I can have that effect on people.

When people say they'll pray for me, I always wonder if they expect me to say, 'Thank you.' Am I supposed to be grateful? It's not like I asked for their prayers and it's certainly not that I need them. I hired the taxi driver to deliver me to my destination on time. I certainly didn't hire him so that I could be delivered from evil along the way. I don't even know what people are asking for in their prayers. Are they praying that I get my voice back? Are they praying that my disability goes away? Good luck with that. Or are they praying that I make it up the stairway to Heaven without the use of a Stannah stairlift?

Whatever you do, please don't pray for me. It's fine. I'm fine. More than fine. I've accepted my situation. It's part of who I am and I'm generally happy with my life, certainly no less happy than most people. I know I'm sometimes hard to understand. I know I have problems drinking. And I know I'm shit at football. Admittedly it's taken a while, but I've finally also accepted that I'm a Geordie. It could be worse – at least I'm not a Mackem.

While I'm dishing out the advice, here's another bit. Always try to give me space. I don't mean that in the emotional sense of the word. I'm being very literal. If you can stop storing all your random junk in the disabled toilet, that would be a great start. But what I mean is that you need to give me room to live my life. Trust that if I want help, I'll say so. And I think that goes for just about everyone with a disability. I'll tell you what works for me. You'll need to carry the drinks to our table, offer your arm when the stairs have no railing, and hold my hand through at least one major medical event. I'm a bit of a coward when it comes to hospitals. If you want to be the hero, that's how to do it. Otherwise, back off and listen. Give my body the room and time it needs. I've lived with my disability all of my life. I know what I'm capable of. And I'm also very independent. So I want to do as much as possible for myself. Yes, it will take me a while to get my clothes off. If you and I ever find ourselves in an undressing situation (very unlikely, I know: you have standards, after all), I'd suggest you watch a movie while you wait.

Probably one of the longer ones. How about *The Lord of the Rings*? All three, back to back, should just about do it. But please don't assume you know best and smother me with your good intentions.

It feels so good to get that off my chest.

GRIM REAPERS ON THE ROYAL MILE

7

B y February 2012, just a few months after my backstage meeting with Ross Noble, I was booked in for my first ever gig as a comedian. I was lucky enough to know someone who ran a successful comedy night in Sunderland and he kindly offered me a ten-minute slot. Brand new comics often get offered shorter spots at established nights to hone their craft. You'll usually find them sandwiched between the professionals who help keep the night running smoothly. I was just in the right place at the right time.

Ten minutes seems like no time at all now, but back then it felt like for ever. I had absolutely no idea what I was going to talk about for ten minutes. I hadn't even given a PowerPoint presentation at work, so this was a big leap for me. The closest I had ever come to being the centre of attention was when I was cast in school plays. And, let's face it, performing in front of your loving parents in a school production of *Oliver!* with all your mates isn't quite in the same league as getting up onstage to a bunch of strangers in a comedy club.

I got to work writing my material, and when I thought it was good enough, I let Nathan read it to see if he liked it too. Thankfully he did, and he would have had no problem telling me if he hadn't, and some of that material is still some of my favourite stuff that I've written. I wheel it out whenever I can. You may have noticed. Even then, despite amazing support, I was so nervous about performing. Not just in case my jokes were shit, but also in case people couldn't understand my talker. I was worried I'd be standing there telling jokes to myself, a whole bunch of bemused people staring back at me. I reasoned that my cerebral palsy might buy me a couple of minutes' grace but then they'd start throwing things. This was Sunderland, after all.

I remember my first gig as if it was half an hour ago, never mind yesterday. It was a Sunday evening and it had been snowing all day, meaning that it was quite an effort for me to get there in the first place. And there was always the chance that the audience wouldn't bother turning out. I couldn't work out if that was a good thing or a bad thing. Despite almost slipping and falling over on the ice several times – and let's not forget that walking isn't my forte in even the most propitious of circumstances – I made it to the venue in one piece. I was lucky enough to have quite a number of friends in the audience, which helped steady the nerves a lot. At least I knew they'd laugh at my material even if it was the worst act they'd ever seen, but as I was walking up on to the stage I still had no idea how it would go.

I received a warm welcome from the small number of people who had braved the weather to come to the gig. This was the moment of truth. Was I going to die on stage or not? I told my first joke and everyone loved it, then my second and they loved that even more. My nerves disappeared as a massive adrenalin rush kicked in from hearing people laugh at jokes I'd written. I was loving every second of it, and suddenly ten minutes didn't seem very long after all. In fact, it didn't seem long *enough* – I wanted more. My set that night was over in a flash, and almost all my material had gone down well. I walked off that stage feeling like a giant.

The buzz of making people laugh is still one of the best feelings there is – you should try it some time – and I first truly experienced it on that snowy Sunday in Sunderland. I didn't sleep that night because I was on such a high. I wanted to do it all again as soon as possible. I had been bitten by the comedy bug, and when it bites, it bites hard.

That first gig in Sunderland was filmed by my friend and work colleague Julie. (Big thanks to her for filming it. Sorry you still haven't received any royalties for your hard work.) You can find it on my YouTube channel, if you like. You're probably wondering who has the arrogance to film their very first gig as a stand-up comedian, right? I don't blame you. In hindsight, it was pretty egotistical of me. After all, it could have gone horrifically badly and I'd have looked like a muppet. Although, if it had, I would just have trashed the camera it was on and I certainly wouldn't have posted it on YouTube. I don't know what I was thinking – this is where the insanity thing comes into play. I guess I just saw that gig as a one-off event, and as it was going to be unique, I wanted to capture it on camera. I'm glad I did.

It's interesting for me to watch it now and see what I was like back then and how much I've changed as a comedian since.

You learn from watching yourself back, excruciating as it can sometimes be. Obviously, I look very nervous on the video. Because I was. Apart from those aforementioned performances in end-of-term plays at school (in one I was cast as a robot; if that isn't typecasting, I don't know what is), I had never stepped on to a stage. So this was a big deal for me. Nowadays I'd like to think I'm a lot more confident onstage and have a much bigger presence up there. I also know how to work the crowd a bit more and give them what they want. The show is more interactive, rather than just being a straight delivery of my material. That could only come with experience, though, and I had none on that night in Sunderland.

It's also interesting to see how much my material has changed since then. Back in 2012, I was all about getting the next laugh as quickly as possible, with short, punchy jokes. Now I feel more comfortable onstage so I don't mind telling a longer story and making the audience wait for the pay-off. I'm also more political, although whether that's my natural habitat, as it were, or simply because the country has gone to shit recently and someone has to say something, I'm not sure. The current government may not be doing anything else right, but they're doing a brilliant job of writing my material for me.

As soon as that first gig was out of the way, I knew I wanted to do another, and as soon as possible. I just didn't know where to start. Thankfully, my mate Nathan came to the rescue again and put me in touch with some gig bookers in Newcastle. The bad news was that I was going to have to wait another month for my next comedy fix. In the meantime, I got to work writing new material to try out and spent time honing the stuff I already had. Unlike other comedians, I had something else to work on: I had to figure out how best to use my talker to tell my jokes.

For my stand-up debut I had used an app called 'Speak It'. It did exactly what its name suggests: it simply spoke whatever I typed. And this worked fine for my first gig because I knew exactly what I was going to say and in which order I'd say it. My set was one long, continuous piece of text, with pauses in between each joke. I soon realized, however, that this method wasn't going to cut it in the long term. I couldn't just stand there, press play and hope for the best. I needed to have a lot more control over my material, what I was going to say and when I was going to say it. After all, the secret of good comedy is . . . timing. Without control of that I was going to be completely screwed.

HEY, HO, PROLOQUO2GO

I hadn't imagined I would have to refine the logistics of my act. After all, my debut gig in Sunderland was supposed to be a one-off. Debut and finale all in one. Mission accomplished. Challenge ticked. But even though I hadn't given any thought to the long term until that point, this was a new problem I was very happy to have. Until then I had only used my talker for day-to-day communication, and I was an expert at using it for that. Now I realized that this wasn't going to work when I was performing comedy (well, unless I had a few hours to spare and a really patient audience). My needs had changed and, just like that, 'Speak It' was redundant. I required something much more flexible. I'd be going to different places with different audiences so I couldn't just rely on having the same set every time. I needed to find an app where I could store all my material as different buttons and just hit each button when I wanted to tell that particular joke – adapting to the audience. I also needed something that made it easy enough to find all my different gags in an instant, as I couldn't be wasting time searching for stuff on stage. *Hang on, I'm going to be funny in just a minute . . .* Surefire way to look like a muppet. Any silence in the room would have killed the momentum of my set and indeed my career. Luckily for me, a smart app like that did exist, and it was called 'Proloquo2Go'. It never gets any easier to say.

I've developed quite a close relationship with the people who make the app since I first started to use it, so I might be a bit biased, but I still think it's one of the best products out there for people with communication difficulties. At the risk of sounding like I'm on the payroll, it's very versatile and puts the user at the heart of the app. If someone has only a basic grasp of vocabulary (a young kid, say), they can use it with basic phrases and even pictures, but it offers advanced users full sentences, complex grammar and more. Basically, it has something to suit everyone's needs. I think I'm the only one who has used it to be a stand-up comedian, but it rises to that challenge as well.

With this problem solved, my next couple of gigs went almost as well as my first. I didn't think anything was ever going to match the buzz I'd felt on making my stand-up comedy debut. It was a moment of pure realization that I could do it. But it still felt really special to be up on that stage making people laugh again.

I was only about five gigs into my budding career as a comedian when I first appeared on television – *BBC Breakfast*, no less. I doubt any other comedian in the early days of their career would have got the coverage that I did, but then again, most other comedians can speak perfectly fine. Having no voice was my USP. It made me unique. It made me stand out from the crowd and got people to take notice of what I was doing. A stand-up comedian who can't speak? Surely not!

Being on *BBC Breakfast* was a very big deal to me, of course, yet I really didn't know what all the fuss was about. I was just doing my thing in a pretty small way, and glad to be doing it. But Matt Lucas was on the *Breakfast* sofa that morning, and after the film about me had finished, he called me a 'wonderful comedian'. I was watching at home. Hearing him say that gave me butterflies.

After that piece aired I started to get offers from further afield. One of my first gigs outside the North East was in Bingley, Yorkshire, and that was closely followed by a trip to Aberdeen. This was all very exciting to me. Before that, I didn't even know where Bingley was. But this presented me with a second problem that I'd never thought I'd have to deal with. How the hell was I going to get to these places and how would I survive while I was there?

CHECKLIST OF THE GODS

One thing I knew for sure was that I couldn't drive myself everywhere, and I couldn't get the train by myself either – I would have fallen down the gap between the train and the platform edge. Even if I could have done the journey, I would still have struggled to take care of myself while I was away. I would need help with getting dressed, brushing my teeth, making my food and so on.

This seems to be a familiar theme but, once again, it was my friends who helped me out. Hawke and Nathan were at the top of what was to become quite a long list of 'gig buddies' – people who would help me get to where I needed to be and look after me while I was there. I'll always be very grateful to them all because, without them, I couldn't have a career as a comedian: the Taxi of Mam and Dad only goes so far. I've always paid each and every one of my gig buddies for all their hard work. I'll be the first to admit that I don't travel light, so they'd often look like packhorses when we got a train together, but no one ever complained. At least, not to my face. In fact, some of them learned not to pack much for themselves to try to ease the load a bit.

With this in mind, it's only fair that they get a mention. It's the least they deserve for carrying my dirty underwear all over the country. So thank you to Nathan, Hawke, Curt, Charlene, the two Laurens, Ricia, Stacey, Emy and everyone else who has helped me along the way. I even roped in Mam and Dad for a few trips. You're all amazing for putting up with me and thank you very much for carrying all of my shit, including:

- My gig T-shirt – to look good on stage
- Jumpers – to keep warm
- Jeans – to look cool
- Underwear – to prevent me from getting charged with indecent exposure

- Socks – with the days of the week on them, obviously
- Pyjamas – I'm not too cool to be comfortable on a night
- Coat – even though I'm a Geordie
- 2 x iPads – you never know when you'll need a second
- 1 phone – an iPhone to keep myself on brand
- A shitload of cables – I'm not sure if I even know what half of them do
- More chargers than I know what to do with – see above
- Kitchen roll – for my messy eating
- Tissues – for my dribbly chin
- Complan – a nutritional milkshake (chocolate obviously) that I drink to help keep my energy levels up. It's hard work being a comedian on the road
- Shaker – to make the aforementioned
- Spoons – to eat
- Beaker – to drink
- Thickener – because I have trouble swallowing, I have this stuff put into my drinks to make the liquid thicker. It tastes rank and I wouldn't recommend trying it. Imagine drinking jelly
- Flannel – to wipe up all the mess I make when I eat
- Shower body wash – because I don't trust that hotel toiletry. How can it wash your hair *and* your body?
- Toothbrush and toothpaste – to protect that winning smile

- Shaver and aftershave – so I look and smell good for the ladies
- Body spray – you get quite smelly when you're standing on a hot stage for any amount of time
- Washing-up liquid – to turn the hotel bathroom into a makeshift kitchen
- Dishcloth – to complete the look described above
- Tea towel – to dry the washing-up that I've just done in the hotel sink
- Food – because I'm a very fussy eater
- Ribena – literally one of the few things that I actually drink
- Mirror – to use when I'm eating so I can see where my mouth is. Also because I'm vain
- Tablets – to stop me collapsing in a heap
- Money – because it talks
- Business cards – because I'm always hustling
- Merchandise – see above

. . . and for managing to keep me upright at the same time.

THE SPREADSHEET HITS THE FAN

Staying upright has always been a problem for me, and my debut season at the Edinburgh Fringe nearly put me six feet under after I contracted pneumonia, then had to spend the next three weeks stuck in a Scottish hospital. To say this was a shame was putting it mildly. This was my first ever festival as a performer, having visited as a punter ever since I was a teenager. To have it cut short by illness was a real sickener in every sense.

Before I became a stand-up comedian, I loved going to the Fringe to watch as many shows as I could. I was one of those people who would triangulate the locations of different venues to maximize my comedy opportunities, seeing five or six shows a day and running (or trying to) from venue to venue for my next comedy fix. Damn you, cobbles! I even planned my itinerary on a spreadsheet. You can't beat a good spreadsheet.

Over the years, I'd dragged up to Edinburgh anyone and everyone who was willing to travel with me. The fact that you could see the likes of Al Murray and Lee Evans in tiny venues alongside some amazing up-and-coming comedians was my idea of a good holiday. In fact, it was at the Fringe that I first saw some of my favourite comedians today – the likes of Tom Binns, Tony Law and John Bishop.

So you can imagine the feeling I had in my heart in 2013, when I took my first show up to Edinburgh. Now that I'm a bit more experienced, I know that anyone can do that if they really want to (if they're crazy enough and if they sell most of their internal organs to pay for it). Back then, I just thought it meant I'd made it. My first show there was at the Stand Comedy Club. I had spent months writing it and making it as good as it could be. When the opening night came around, I was bursting with pride and excitement. My venue held just forty people but every single one of them made my first Fringe appearance very special. Here I was, performing at the biggest arts festival in the world, alongside some of the best-known names on the comedy circuit, and I was so excited.

At least, I was excited for the first week or so. My shows were going well, I was getting good reviews and I was having the time of my life. I couldn't have asked for more. I should have known that something would go wrong sooner or later. When it did, it was in a spectacular fashion.

I'm sure that many comedians have gone up to the festival and died on their arses, metaphorically. But I'm probably one of the few who have come offstage and nearly died literally. Actually, come to think of it, given the prevailing levels of alcohol consumption, maybe not. Either way, it was a huge kick in the balls. But I should have expected it. My body likes to bring me down to earth with a bump when I'm enjoying myself most. It's almost as if it's decided that, just when things are looking good and I'm feeling good, it's important to remind me that I'm disabled. I'd had a warning on the very first night of my Edinburgh run, when a mixture of nerves, stress and the fact that my venue was boiling hot triggered one of my most memorable epileptic incidents.

I was about fifty minutes into my show when I felt it coming on. I started to panic because I couldn't do anything about it. I didn't want to injure myself but I didn't want to have to stop the show either. Amazingly, on this occasion, I managed to keep it at bay (although I can't remember the last ten minutes of the show). My mam was in the audience and she said I had a glazed look on my face and somehow went into autopilot. I still have no idea how I stopped myself having a full-on fit. But it's a little worrying that she couldn't tell the difference between me doing the show as a well person and me doing the show in shut-down mode.

I really did become ill a couple of weeks later. Afterwards I found out that I had 'hit the Edinburgh wall'. This is what most comedians do after about their third week at the Fringe. And it makes sense, because as great an experience as doing a show at the biggest comedy festival in the world is, it takes it out of you mentally and physically. Looking on the bright side, though, as a consequence of what happened to me up there, I now know how to spell 'pneumonia'.

It all started after one of my Saturday-night shows. I'd had pains in my stomach all day and they got worse during the gig. In fact, I'm surprised I didn't collapse onstage and roll around on the floor. Not because it was hurting that much, I'm just an attention-seeking bastard who doesn't like to miss an opportunity. Eventually, a few hours later, the pains were so bad that I had to ring for an ambulance. That was easier said than done. The first two times I tried, the operator assumed I must be some sort of automated message trying to sell them insurance and hung up on me.

Somehow the ambulance managed to find where I was staying – it was the back end of beyond and even *I* hardly knew where it was – and I thought I'd finally be getting some decent pain relief. But I was wrong. It just so happened that the ambulance men recognized me from somewhere and spent the next ten minutes trying to figure out who I was. From where I was standing or, rather, from where I was doubled over, writhing in pain, there were some more pressing issues. But part of me was loving the fact that they knew who I was. I suspect most comedians would say exactly the same thing. You don't get up onstage and try to make people laugh without having a massive ego.

Eventually, the medics got to the bottom of the key issue of my identity – as some bloke they'd seen perform a comedy act somewhere – and gave me some morphine, like it was a reward for amusing them. The relief was immense. Morphine is one of those drugs where it's almost worth getting ill just to try some. Not that I'm advocating drug use, of course, but, honestly, you must try it before you die. Just try not to leave it too close to the wire when you're so far gone you can't enjoy it.

If you've been to the Edinburgh Fringe then you'll know that the Royal Mile is a very weird place at the best of times. There's always some nutter dressed up as something crazy, doing stuff that's really insane, which he shamelessly calls a performance and for which behaviour in any other setting he'd be sectioned. So, consider what it was like for me to be driven through the centre of Edinburgh, completely off my face on morphine, with all that going on around me. I have never been so freaked out.

At one point I saw a group of men dressed as Grim Reapers ambling down the Royal Mile. And, let's be honest, when you're on the way to hospital, feeling temporarily better because of the morphine but still knowing that something is seriously wrong with you, you really don't want to see the Grim Reaper chasing after you. In a total cliché, your life flashes before your eyes, and you suddenly remember you haven't done any washing lately and are about to die wearing dirty underwear.

Luckily, I made it to hospital with my heart still beating, but with my underwear even dirtier than when I'd left home. As it was a weekend, I was seen by the out-of-hours doctor. Much as I respect and have cause to be grateful to the NHS, the truth is that the out-of-hours medics are sometimes those who aren't quite good enough to work on weekdays and – as it turned out in this case – have little bedside manner. These are the sort of doctors who enjoy watching *Casualty* and playing the board game *Operation*, then think they know everything. My doctor looked like the farmer in *Babe*, which was appropriate, because he would definitely have been more suited to looking after animals.

Before you start to think that maybe I'm being unfairly tough on an overworked medic, let me tell you what happened.

At this point we didn't know what was wrong with me. So he helpfully suggested that my pain might be a result of the way I walk. Yes, that's right. The way I've walked all my life. The way I've walked all my life without getting a pain in my stomach. Well done, Doctor. That's obviously the reason why I'm in agony. It's just taken me thirty-two years to realize things aren't quite right.

If that wasn't bad enough, he did an impression of my walk. Yes, he walked like a disabled person to show me that I walk like a disabled person. Because until that point, I honestly had no idea I walked like a disabled person. None at all. His demonstration really helped open my eyes.

Eventually, after I had been poked and prodded half to death, I was diagnosed and put on a ward to be looked after properly rather than by that joker. Most of my fellow patients were quite literally knocking on Heaven's door. By the look of things, some of them hadn't even bothered to knock and had just barged straight in. I was there a long time, and I started to miss the festival after a while. But being in hospital is a lot like being at a festival anyway. It costs loads to park your car, the overcrowding makes it hard to get any sleep, everyone's on drugs, and everyone leaves with more infections than they arrived with.

'Would you like a microphone?'

One of my favourite things about the comedy circuit is
the accidental awkwardness that many of my fellow
comics seem to experience when they're around me. It's
a source of great amusement to me and everyone else in
the green room. I've lost count of the number of times
I've been asked by the compère if I need the
microphone. Newsflash: I can't talk – of course I don't
need the bloody microphone! My talker plugs directly
into the sound desk instead. Other acts have fallen foul
of trying to give me the mic as I walk on to the stage. I
can't imagine how stupid they must feel as I look at
them blankly and introduce myself to the audience
using my talker.

My absolute favourite instance of this happening to
me was during the final of *Britain's Got Talent*, just after
I had been announced as the winner. Dec came over to
ask how I was feeling and tried to hand me the mic so
that I could tell everyone how delighted I was. If you
watch it back you can see the exact point that he
realizes what he's done. The smirk on his face as he
tries not to laugh live on national television is a joy to
behold.

Then there are the compères who get my name
wrong. I've been Lost Voice Boy, No Voice Man, The

Boy With No Speech and everything in between. On several occasions, I've even been introduced as Lee Rigby, the name of the soldier who tragically fell victim to a brutal Islamist murder on the streets of south-east London in 2013 – a bit of a mood-killer, to say the least.

A RIGHT OLD PRO

8

I've been on the comedy circuit for about seven years now. Life as a comedian hasn't always been a bed of roses. It would have been pretty boring if it had, to be honest. And I don't think it's ever that easy for anyone. It's not a career for the faint-hearted. It is, however, a very good career for the insane.

My comedy career has taken me all over the place. I've played in some lovely venues but some shit-holes as well. Not that I ever get to see anything much of the town I'm visiting. It's dark when I arrive and it's even darker when I leave. And I say that partly by way of a disclaimer: if I lay into the places that have hosted me they'll never invite me back. Suffice to say some gigs are more memorable than others, for both good and bad reasons.

1. *My first gig at the Stand Comedy Club in Newcastle.*
   After having watched comedy there as a punter since the venue had opened a few years previously, I couldn't believe that I was actually going to be

performing on the same stage. I was still a relatively new comedian at the time, so I was still quite raw when it came to being a comic. I honestly wasn't sure if I was good enough to be appearing at the Stand yet. Not that it seemed to matter to any of the staff or the other comedians on the bill that night. From the moment I stepped into that green room, I was treated with so much respect and decency. The staff were so helpful and friendly that it really did feel like home straight away. For me, that's a sign of a really good comedy club, and I think their positive attitude towards both comics and customers alike is why it's my favourite venue in the country. The audience was lovely as well (it turns out they always are); everything was just perfect. The Stand in Newcastle really is my second home.

2. *The strip club in Birmingham.* This is the only time I've ever been to a strip club in my life. Honest, Mam. And after this particular experience, I'm in no hurry to go back. Of course it wasn't being used as a strip club while I was performing (although I was told to keep my set short as the girls were getting ready for the actual strip club to open later), it was just a comedy night that was using a strip club as a venue. Not that this made it any better. Comedy in strip clubs doesn't work. The lighting is all wrong because it's set up to show off dancing girls, not middle-aged comedians, the sound system is terrible, and everything you touch seems to be sticky. They didn't even take down the pole that the girls dance

around while we were performing. I wasn't sure whether to tell jokes or do my best slut-drop.

3. *The British Library*. I once did a charity gig in the foyer. That was – how to explain it? – *different*! All of my life I had been told not to talk in the library, yet there I was breaking all the rules. I am quite child-ishly proud that I got to say the words 'bastard', 'fuck' and even to drop the C-bomb in the British Library without being told to shush.

4. *Breakneck Comedy, Aberdeen*. My trip to Aberdeen was one of my first gigs outside the North East (and also the first I was actually getting paid to do! Happy days). It was a pretty big deal to me. A heady mix-ture of nerves and excitement hit me on the train on the way up as I wondered how it would go. In the end, it was a fantastic gig, if I say so myself. Still one of my best ever. From the moment I walked onstage, the audience just seemed to connect with every joke. It was like I could say nothing wrong. For a new comedian, that was such an amazing feeling. I've been back to Breakneck Comedy in Aberdeen quite a few times since and I always have a lovely time there. Obviously we must share a similar sense of humour as there's no question the audience is up for a good laugh and everyone is always thrilled to see me. At the back of my mind lurks the dark thought that it's so far north they'd be pleased to see anyone, but I'll push that away.

5. *The Comedy Store, London*. This is the Holy Grail. Most comedians have ambitions to perform on this

stage because it's probably the best-known comedy venue in the country. Admittedly, my first gig here was by default because that was where the BBC New Comedy Award was held, but I've been back since entirely legitimately and have loved it every time . . . even though there are a lot of stairs to go down to reach it. No falls yet, touch wood.

6. *Supporting Ross Noble at the Stand, Newcastle.* Getting to be the support act for my favourite comedian in my favourite venue, which was sold out, was a very special moment indeed. Especially as he'd asked me to do it himself via a message on Twitter, which came totally out of the blue. I even did a Ross Noble impression just to get him back for doing Stephen Hawking years earlier. And when I say 'impression', I mean I played a recording of his voice on my talker. It's the same thing.

7. The Gadget Show *at the Glee Club in Birmingham.* For some reason, *The Gadget Show* was filming a robot that could tell jokes. They also thought it would be a good idea to book me for the same show . . . because, you know, that isn't even a bit insensitive. We were like a robot version of Morecambe and Wise. The good news is that it turns out robots can't tell jokes and I am funnier than a machine.

8. *The Black Box in Belfast.* My first international gig (I got on a plane and went over some water, so it definitely counts, however much the ghost of Ian Paisley might disagree with me). I was really excited for this one and it didn't disappoint. Belfast is such a friendly city and welcomed me with open arms.

9. *The gig in a beer garden in December.* As cold as it sounds. A lovely show but even with the heaters on everyone froze their bits off. Needless to say, I didn't wear one of my T-shirts for this one. At least everyone was shaking as much as I was for once.

10. *CarFest, Cheshire.* Imagine being introduced on a stage in a huge field by Chris Evans with over fifty thousand people watching you, then having Status Quo come on after you, all to raise money for Children In Need. Tick. Tick. Tick. Tick. I still can't believe it happened.

11. *The gig for Sunderland City Council.* It may surprise you to know that I don't always swear at my gigs. I do have a clean set for when the need arises. I just have to remember to hit the right buttons on my talker. On this occasion I failed at that task and said 'fuck' in front of the Mayor of Sunderland. I think I got away with it because I'm disabled.

After a few years of being on the comedy circuit, I had become relatively successful (and by that I mean I didn't have to get the bargain-basement Megabus to my gigs any more). At the same time, I was still holding down a job as part of the communications team (yes, I know, stop giggling at the back) at Sunderland City Council. Quite simply, I was burning the candle at both ends – coming home from gigs in the early hours of the morning, then getting up to go to work at 6 a.m. I coped with it for the first couple of years, fuelled by adrenalin, but then it started to get too much. My job at the council was demanding enough on its own, so when I started to get more and more work as a comedian, I ended up not having much downtime at all. The result was that my work in both areas suffered. I couldn't give either the attention they deserved so I always tried to work myself harder to make up for that.

I began to realize that something had to give, and as much as I enjoyed my time at the council, it was stand-up comedy that had my heart.

The council was always 100 per cent supportive of my adventures in comedy and tried to accommodate me as much as they could. I'm still very appreciative of that, because I dread to think what life would have been like if they hadn't given me some flexibility. I probably wouldn't have had a moment to myself – and I know that life is like that for all new comedians and even those who are pretty well established. But having cerebral palsy does add a few extra complications. The day job pays the bills, but sustaining the day job takes its toll.

Luckily, in my last few years at the council, they allowed me to go part time, and I worked one day a week at home as well. This eased the pressure, but it was still pretty stressful trying to juggle two demanding jobs – especially when these hands are shit at juggling anyway.

It was 2014. As the day job started to take a back seat, I decided to enter the BBC New Comedy Award – a competition that Radio 4 holds every year to find the best up-and-coming comedians. I don't want to sound ungrateful, but in general I'm not really a big fan of stand-up comedy competitions. I don't think you can judge someone fairly on seeing just a couple of minutes of their material, but when I looked at some of the other acts who had won this in the past – Peter Kay, Sarah

Millican and Lee Mack among them – I thought it was worth a shot. It would be a great experience if nothing else.

My heat for the competition was in Edinburgh during the Fringe and somehow I managed to get through it. Then, in November, my semi-final was at the 99 Club in London, and somehow I managed to get through that as well. I just couldn't believe what was happening. The final was held at London's Comedy Store in December.

By this point I wasn't really getting nervous at gigs any more. I knew I probably should be, but the nerves had fallen away, and it just seemed natural for me to be up on that stage telling gags. But at the Comedy Award final, I was completely shitting my pants. It didn't help that the green room at the Comedy Store is rather small. Six very nervous comedians were pacing around a very small room, undoubtedly making each other feel more nervous, purely by being in the same tight space. I think I was third on the bill that night and I reasoned that I might feel a bit better after I'd been onstage and my set was out of the way.

I was wrong. The waiting around for the verdict just made me feel worse. I had achieved so much just by getting this far, and I wanted it all to be over. About an hour after I'd come offstage it was time for the results to be announced.

How on the edge of my seat was I at this point? Well, the answer is not very. Whenever I'm performing onstage, I always have a table to put my talker on. So the surprise that I had won the whole competition was slightly spoiled for me because the producer had asked for the table to be moved back onstage for the results. I knew then that I had either won or that this was the cruellest bluff ever – someone having a brilliant laugh at the expense of a disabled man. A risky move, I thought, until it was confirmed that it was the former, not the latter, when the producer came into the green room and asked me if I had my winner's speech ready. Well, of course I did. One thing about using a talker to speak with is that you have to be prepared for every eventuality, however unlikely it seems. A few moments later, when my name was read out as the winner, I might not have looked as surprised as I should (and UK Adult Male Graham definitely wasn't giving anything away), but I was bloody chuffed.

WRITING ABILITY

The kudos of winning the BBC New Comedy Award wasn't my only prize. I also got the opportunity to write a sitcom pilot for Radio 4. I had always enjoyed listening to comedy on Radio 4 and some of my idols, such as *The League of Gentlemen*, had started off with a series on the station. I already had a few ideas for potential sitcoms and I was very excited to get started on the project.

At the same time it was quite daunting. Obviously I had never written comedy for radio before and I knew it would be very different from writing my stand-up material. For a start, I wouldn't be writing on my own any more. Other people would be involved with the script. Another massive difference was that I'd be writing lines for characters and not just stuff I could say onstage. It needed to have a storyline. I was up for the challenge, though.

Luckily, the BBC paired me with a writing partner – someone who had done this before and, unlike me, knew what they were doing. Katherine Jakeways and I seemed to hit it off as soon as we met. We bounced ideas off each other and ended up with what was to become my first radio sitcom – *Ability*. I'm very thankful that I had Katherine in my corner. I learned so much from both her and our producer, Jane Berthoud, and they made the experience of writing a whole sitcom a lot less scary.

Ability is about a disabled bloke, called Matt, who can't speak and can be a bit of a dickhead at times. He's purely fictional, obviously. He lives with his best mate, Jess, and has a very dodgy carer called Bob (inspired by my very own dodgy carer, the one who fell asleep on the floor, pissed out of his head). It's a story about how, together, they try to use Matt's disability to their advantage, and you can probably guess that things don't always go to plan. In the first series alone, Matt has become a drug-dealer, tried shoplifting just to see if he can get away with it, and set up a robot sex line called Dial-A-Sexbot. I'd like to say that my life is just as exciting as Matt's but, sadly, it isn't.

Someone other than my mam liked it enough to recommission it. And I'm glad about that because I've really enjoyed writing it. Long may it continue. *The Archers* should watch out. I liked the fact that it took me out of my comfort zone and made me think about writing differently for a new medium. I enjoyed being able to bounce the characters off each other in a way that I could never do with my stand-up. When I'm on stage, I'm talking directly to the audience and, in the absence of any hecklers, it's very much a one-way conversation. With a sitcom there's the opportunity to have dialogue between a few characters and I liked having the freedom to create a situation out of my own funny ideas. Which is why they call it situation comedy, I guess.

The idea of my 'inner voice' first came about when we were writing *Ability*. We thought it would be nice for Matt to have a proper Geordie voice as well as the voice of his talker, his Graham. And we realized that Matt would probably think in this voice as well. This 'inner voice' really helps to add an extra dimension to the sitcom. Matt's thoughts are as important to the storyline as what he says out loud. It gives the listener an insight into Matt's life as a disabled person that we don't often get to hear . . . unless you're smart enough to be reading this book, of course. I just hope you never get the chance to hear what I'm really thinking or I'll be in a lot of trouble.

We were very lucky to have a great cast for *Ability*. Everyone turned out to be perfect for their roles. Of course, because I'm an attention-seeking whore, I cast myself as Matt, although there wasn't much competition for the role of 'guy with cerebral palsy who uses a talker to speak with'. I think I have that niche market pretty much sewn up, for the time being at least.

I was particularly chuffed to have Allan Mustafa (who plays MC Grindah in BBC Three's *People Just Do Nothing*) playing Matt's useless carer, Bob. I was already a big fan of his so I was thrilled when he agreed to take the part. Working alongside him in the studio was a lot of fun and I think he made Bob even better than we'd written him. His little ad-libs during the recording of the show gave the character the extra edge he needed to come across as a truly dodgy bloke who was also quite lovable. At the risk of sounding like a luvvie, it was a joy to work with him. In fact, the whole cast and crew had such a laugh together and it was incredible to be part of that. I definitely want to do more stuff like this. So, if you're looking for 'guy with cerebral palsy who uses a talker to speak with' for your next television or radio project, I'm available.

Hearing *Ability* on Radio 4 for the first time was a great moment. Because I had been gigging at the Stand in Newcastle on the night it was first broadcast, I was lucky enough to be able to hear it on the venue's sound system after the gig had finished. I loved listening to it surrounded by all my mates from the Stand. It seemed very fitting after all the support they'd given me over the years.

Winning the New Comedy Award not only meant that I must be a decent comedian after all (the award is judged by both the comedy industry and the general public, which is a nice endorsement), it was also a watershed moment for me personally. For the first time since I'd started doing comedy I began to believe that maybe this wasn't just a very time-consuming and exhausting hobby and that I could actually earn a living by making people laugh.

Even so, it was still a while before I could take things further. Before I got my job at the council, I had struggled for three years to find any employment at all. I was getting plenty of interviews but none were getting me anywhere. I'd like to think it was because almost everyone was going through a tough time back then. The banking crisis had just devastated the economy so each job vacancy was getting hundreds of applicants. But, at the back of my mind, I did wonder whether my disability was holding me back. The paranoid part of my brain is very good at working overtime (rather ironic when I couldn't even get a job), so it was hard to shake the feeling that I was being discriminated against. For a start, just imagine how many risk-assessment forms you need to fill in before employing me!

The job I eventually got was online content manager for Sunderland City Council. As with most jobs at the council, its title was a mouthful, but it basically meant that I was responsible for all the content on the council's website. Writing stories about bin collections never did get any less mundane but after a long time of struggling to find work, despite my master's degree, I was happy to be doing it.

In the previous interview before the one for this job, my talker had decided to play up right in the middle. It started making weird noises and not speaking properly. It was very awkward and I thought it was a sign that maybe I should give up. So when I went for my interview at Sunderland I wasn't expecting much. In fact, on my way home I didn't think I'd done very well. I wrote it off straight away and tried to make myself feel better by convincing myself that I didn't want to be travelling to Sunderland every day on the Metro anyway. So it took me by surprise when I was offered the position. This was to be my first – and so far, at least, only – proper job.

METRO NOT SEXUAL

The rhythm of paid employment took a lot of getting used to. For a start, I was used to being unemployed and lying in. Suddenly I needed to get up at six and be in the office for nine (my morning cleanliness rituals have always taken me longer than they do people who don't have cerebral palsy, for some reason).

It was also my first time using public transport for any length of time. I'd got buses before but not often. Now I had to get the Metro to Sunderland every day. Some of the sights I saw and most of the people I met on those trains proved to be great material for my stand-up routines. Like they say, everything is copy.

Travelling on the Metro also meant I got really good at knowing how to make people get out of the priority seats so I could sit down. My technique of wobbling on my feet just enough to make the other person feel nervous and awkward enough to give up their seat for me was always guaranteed to work. Admittedly, sometimes I overdid it and ended up falling on my arse by accident, but that just made them feel even worse. I was in a win-win situation. It's a bit like the way pregnant women lightly rest their hands on the swell as a subtle reminder to comfy commuters to get the fuck up. You have to work with what you've got.

Getting into a routine was hard. For the first few months of my job, I was exhausted by the time I got home and had to have more than my fair share of early nights just to enable me to cope.

Eventually, my role was expanded to looking after the council's social media as well. Let me tell you, nothing is more depressing than seeing some constantly angry resident tweet about the bad state of potholes at 11 p.m., just as you're about to go to bed. Dealing with angry residents helped build my tolerance of bullshit, though. In fact, I think I'm better at dealing (and mostly ignoring) trolls on social media now because of my experience with them while at the council. I had no choice but to bite my tongue back then – I would definitely have got the sack if I'd told someone to 'fuck off and get a life' from @SunderlandUK.

It wasn't all moaning and groaning. I did get to cover some amazing events while at the council. The Sunderland International Airshow was always a highlight . . . when the weather was nice, anyway. The local elections were fun to cover as well (believe it or not). I enjoyed the pressure of having to think on my feet and get something online as quickly as possible. That adrenalin rush is part of the reason why I trained to be a journalist in the first place.

I didn't have to have any adaptations at work to allow me to do my job. Obviously, I was shit at answering the telephone so I tried to stick with communicating through email as much as I could. I was lucky to work with a really great team. We all got on well and I'm still friends with most of them now. Of course, there's always going to be one or two colleagues who prove the exception to the rule. Such as 'Steve' (definitely not his real name), who was in another department and never quite grasped that I wasn't deaf as well as unable to speak. He'd write notes whenever he needed to talk to me instead of just talking. This went on for six years! I just didn't have the heart to tell him.

Working in the public sector also meant that we wasted a lot of money on pointless team-building exercises. One particular occasion sticks in my mind. We were having a team awayday at Derwent Hill, a centre in the Lake District that offers people the chance to do a range of outdoor activities, such as rock-climbing, hill-walking and orienteering. Some of you are already probably thinking it may be a bad idea to take a disabled guy to a place like this, right? But in the interests of bonding with my team (who, I should add, I liked) I went along anyway.

Things started off quite well. Our team won the orienteering task and I was allowed to sit out the rope challenge over the not unreasonable fear that I might hang myself by accident. Then it came to canoeing. It seemed simple enough. It was a two-person canoe so all I had to do was sit there while the other person did all the work. What I wasn't expecting was to be sat cramped on my knees in a canoe for two hours while freezing my arse off in the middle of an icy cold lake in February. I only really noticed there was a problem when I went to climb out and found that my legs had decided to seize up (partly because of the cold and partly because I'd been cutting off the circulation for so long). I couldn't walk at all. Instead, my work colleagues had to take it in turns to help carry me back to the accommodation – an extra exercise in both team-building and trust. It was almost like someone had planned it.

Yet here I was a few years later, willing to leave this glamorous life behind to follow my comedy dreams. Did I really want to give up a well-paid job just to dick around onstage for a living? It was a question I asked myself over and over again. It's a question anyone putting themself out there and taking risks has to ask. I'm not sure if I ever got a concrete answer. My family weren't sure what I should do either.

Being the sensible, level-headed one, my dad thought it was a bad idea to quit the council. I had a secure job with a good pension and I would be silly to throw that away, he said. He was being a good dad, trying to keep things in perspective and my feet on the ground. I'm really glad he was there to do that. Without his wise words I would probably have done something much more impulsive a lot sooner. It definitely helped to have him keep my head in the real world while I was toying with my fantasy world options.

My mam was a bit more open to the idea of me following my dreams, but she still had her reservations . . . or maybe she just wanted her little boy to stay at home a bit more, rather than travel all around the country.

It took a few months of umming and aahing (not literally, of course: I can't umm or aah), but I finally made my decision. That night I sent a group email to my family to explain why I was doing what I was doing.

Hi family,

I'm just emailing you all to let you know that I plan to hand my notice in at the council in the next week or so. It hasn't been an easy decision and I've spent months changing my mind about it, but I've come to the conclusion that there'll never be a right time to do it. If I don't do it now, I feel like I might never do it at all.

There are a few main reasons why I have taken this decision. Firstly, I feel increasingly like I'm struggling to cope with having two careers. If I'm honest, I'm not doing justice to either job because of the amount of work involved in each of them. I feel that something has to give. Even if I do fail and it does end up badly, I'd like to say that I tried. At the moment, I feel as if I can't give comedy my best shot because I'm getting distracted every other day, and when I do get time to myself, I'm usually travelling or trying to recover from a late night. Opportunities to write sitcoms and make a name for myself don't come along every day. I'd like to be able to devote all my time to doing the best that I can to take advantage of them.

This leads me on to my second reason. I don't think my current workload is doing my health any good at all, especially as I hardly have time to relax/go swimming, which used to help a great deal. I could just try not to book as many gigs but then that would mean I wouldn't ever progress at doing something that I love. I would always have a leg in each camp. This isn't who I am. I've always been determined to succeed at whatever I do. Once again, I'd like to see how far I can go.

I've done the sums and I make an average £550 each month from gigging after all my expenses and bills have been taken into account. I realize that I might not always have my benefit money or whatever, but then again I might start making more from comedy as well. No one can tell with any certainty what will happen in the future, that's what makes this all so scary. I've always been sensible with my money, I'll just have to make sure I keep doing that.

Most of all, I think I've reached a massive crossroads in my life. I could concentrate on comedy and writing and everything that comes with it, or I could just keep doing what I'm doing now and never ever reach my full potential. If I don't try to follow my dreams and do what I love doing now, I feel like I'll regret it for the rest of my life.

I hope you all at least understand my reasoning. I owe everything I have achieved so far to all of you. When it comes down to it, I just want to do the best that I can and make you proud of me.

Love you lots,

Lee xxx

So, I quit my job at the council but, award-winner or not, I still had to work my arse off on the comedy circuit to try to establish myself. That's hard enough for an able-bodied comedian, never mind a comedian with cerebral palsy.

Some people still aren't ready to laugh at disability, however funny we try to make it. When I first started doing comedy, you could sometimes hear the gasp from the audience when I walked onstage and they realized I wasn't their usual type of comedian. Okay, so maybe I was (and still am!) white, male and heterosexual, but just not in the way they were expecting. Then their minds were totally blown when the penny dropped that I couldn't speak either. At a gig in Halifax a woman stood up and walked out as soon as I got on to the stage, loudly exclaiming, 'Oh, I can't watch this!' Bear in mind that I hadn't said a word at this point, and you'll be able to see what I'm up against sometimes. The cheeky cow then had the outright nerve to try to shake my hand after the gig had gone well and say, 'Well done.' Needless to say, I took great pleasure in ignoring her.

Whether you like them or not, heckles are part and parcel of the comedy scene. Audience members (mainly drunk audience members) just can't resist hogging some of the limelight and trying to join in with the show. While they think they're hilarious, it's usually the case that they're not. Dealing with heckles is tough for any comedian, but it gets that bit more difficult when you don't really have the ability to interact with the people sitting right in front of you, which is how it is for me. I can't simply stop what I'm saying, deal quickly and brilliantly (I hope) with a drunken punter in the audience, then get back on track. I'm thinking what I'd like to say, but the technology I use isn't that advanced yet. In fact, I often make a joke in my shows about it in the hope of heading people off at the pass: 'Please don't heckle me. If you do we'll be here all night.'

That isn't strictly true, of course. While I may not be able to respond to a heckle in the same way that a speaking comedian does, I still have my own way of dealing with these situations. Of course I do. Like I say, in my situation you always have to be prepared. So if I'm ever heckled, I have some comebacks stored just in case. I'm not expecting any awards for this, but one of them is just 'Shut the fuck up!' It's not clever but should go down a storm in Graham's voice. I have some smarter comebacks as well. The thing is – and this may be tempting Fate – I've never had the chance to use any of them because I'm still waiting for my first heckle.

It's interesting that I've been doing comedy for seven years now and still haven't been subjected to one traditional old-school 'Get off!' type heckle. Most comedians have to put up with them from day one. I don't know for sure why people don't heckle me. But I do have my theories.

The first is that I don't think many people find it socially acceptable to heckle a disabled person. You wouldn't shout at a disabled person in the street (unless you were an absolute dickhead), and I think this same reasoning transfers to when we're on the stage. In a way, I really want someone to heckle me. Not only so I can find out how I would cope with it, but also so I can see how the rest of the audience reacts. That's a social experiment I would be up for taking part in. Suffice to say, I don't think the heckler would come out of it very well.

Another reason why I think I don't get heckled is because of the uniqueness of my act. Whether by accident or on purpose, audiences tend to listen to me a little more than they do with other comedians. It goes without saying that they need to listen more closely to the words I'm saying because they can't rely too much on my tone of voice and body language. So, in a way, I have much more control over an audience because they have no choice but to listen hard. There's expectation on people's faces: they're eager to know what happens next. For someone like me who has struggled to communicate for most of his life, it's pretty weird to have the tables turned in my favour. While once I found it hard to be heard at all, now I have everyone hanging on my every word.

'Can you manage the stairs?'

Something that really gets to me is how inaccessible most comedy venues are. I've lost count of the times I've had to struggle up a steep flight of dilapidated stairs to a room above a pub, or almost fall down some slippery steps into a basement just to make people laugh. I understand that this quirk of architecture is part and parcel of the comedy scene – some of my best gigs have been in that sort of room, where the audience is up close and personal and you can only relax once you've acquainted yourself with the location of the nearest fire exit, just in case.

Comedy thrives in these places – it's almost as though you've been given permission to laugh louder underground or in a low-ceilinged attic – and that's what keeps the industry alive. I just wish that it wasn't always such a faff to get into the venue. The Edinburgh Fringe is especially bad for this. Of course, there's only so much you can do when you hold a comedy festival in one of the oldest cities in the country, but there has to be a happy medium. Comedy is made for everyone so everyone should be able to access it. Things are getting better in some ways, but there's still a lot more that could be done. Accessible venues with accessible toilets would be a good start, but I'd also like to see more input from the disabled community into the running of these festivals and venues. It's no longer good enough that we're just an afterthought. We need to be involved at every stage of the process for progress to be made. Like I said, it's about getting the balance right.

As a disabled comedian, it's especially disheartening when I turn up to the venue and it's inaccessible. That's not only because I'm a lazy bastard who can't be bothered with stairs, but because it also means that some of the people who've paid to see me might not be able to get in either. I do feel very guilty when people tweet me saying they were disappointed that they couldn't get in to see me perform. But, most of the time, it's out of my hands, especially in Edinburgh where I can only afford to play certain venues without remortgaging my house. I'd love to be in a position where I can pick and choose my venue in the city but at the moment I'm not. There needs to be an overarching change in how accessible comedy festivals are, and it has to come from the top down.

The comedy circuit also needs to make itself more accessible in other ways. There are some great disabled comedians on the circuit, but only a handful of them seem to get booked by the bigger clubs. This is a massive shame and people are missing out on seeing some excellent acts because of it. So, go on, guys and girls, try booking some more of us. You won't catch anything, I promise.

HAS BRITAIN GOT TALENT?

9

I n my early years as a comedian, people used to ask me why I didn't go on *Britain's Got Talent*. And they had a point. On the face of it, I was exactly the type of performer who should have suited the show. I had a unique act, I had one hell of a back-story and, most of all, I lived in Britain and was talented. To my friends, it was a no-brainer. I guess the truth is that in the early days I just didn't see it as a route I wanted to go down. Comedians used to think that *Britain's Got Talent* were three dirty words that should never be spoken, and looked down their noses at it. Yes, me too. This was watered-down entertainment for the masses and we were all too cool for that. I was very wary of getting known as 'that bloke off *Britain's Got Talent*'. And, yes, I'm now fully aware that I'll always be 'that bloke who won *Britain's Got Talent*' . . . or *The X Factor* . . . or *The*

Voice. It depends which member of the general public you're talking to.

Another thing that bothered me was that I'd have to tone down my jokes if I was going to tell them on television before the watershed in front of millions of families eating their tea. And the southerners eating their dinner. My sense of humour is really dark at times . . . and I fucking love swearing. That's just the sort of person I am. I'm used to being able to swear in my act. I think it helps make the whole act funnier. Not only because you've got a posh accent saying words like 'fuck' and 'bollocks' – works a treat every time – but also because I genuinely believe that some of my material works a lot better with swear words in. They act as punctuation.

I've come to this conclusion through experience. I've done a lot of charity gigs where I haven't been allowed to swear and, although the jokes have still gone down well with the audience, they just don't seem to hit home in the same way. When I'm allowed to swear, the punch-lines seem to have more impact. I've always had a reputation for being a little close to the bone – I know I can get away with it because of my disability – so I was worried about losing my edginess by going on *Britain's Got Talent* and I wasn't sure if that was a sacrifice I was willing to make. I enjoy shocking an audience and making them think a bit more about subjects they might normally ignore – if disability doesn't touch your life directly you may not spend much time considering it.

But to create a set that was right for *Britain's Got Talent* it wasn't just a case of replacing the naughty words with a nicer alternative. Yes, that would work in some cases: 'wanker' could become 'idiot'; 'shit' could become 'poo'. But I would also have to write some brand-new family-friendly material especially for the show. If my watered-down and sanitized material wasn't good enough, if the laughs weren't loud enough, then my decision to audition might prove to have been a huge mistake.

A number of factors helped me change my mind to do the show in 2018. The first thing was that comedy has become a lot more popular on *Britain's Got Talent* in recent years after the success of the likes of Daliso Chaponda and Jonny Awsum. Gone are the days when it was all about terrible singers and dancing dogs (and, let's be honest, anyone would have been gutted to be beaten by a foxtrotting canine). There is now much more variety on the show and stand-up comedy has become an integral part of that. If it wasn't for Jonny and Daliso sticking their necks on the line and giving it a go in the first place, I doubt I would have convinced myself to do it at all. I like to think I'm pretty brave, pretty up for things, but I'm not a fool. If I do something, I like to know I've got a serious shot at doing it well. So, the way was paved.

Second, when you've been doing comedy for as long as I have, you begin to realize that the opportunities for real television exposure (more than just a brief news magazine feature on an interesting act by a disabled comic) are few and far between. That's true for everyone (even truer for those who aren't lucky enough to be disabled). And there's a lot of competition. Yes, there's *Live at the Apollo* and other shows of a similar ilk that give up-and-coming comedians a certain amount of exposure but, brilliant as they are, even they don't get the viewing figures they once did. In contrast, *Britain's Got Talent* is event television. Millions of people still watch each episode, and that's not counting those who see clips – of the best and worst bits – on the various social-media platforms.

So, to me, it began to make sense from that point of view: I knew that however well I did on the programme, even if I made just one appearance, the level of exposure I would get could only be a good thing. I just had to keep in mind that a lot of the *Britain's Got Talent* audience might not be my target market – my most recent Edinburgh show has a game in it called 'Play Your Crips Right'! (Have I mentioned that I like to be a bit challenging about disability?) But I didn't see that as such a bad thing either. As long as people are enjoying your comedy, who cares about demographics? Making people laugh is the key thing. If my *Britain's Got Talent* experience has taught me anything, it's that it's possible to find people who like what you do in some of the unlikeliest places. Those people would never have found out about me if it wasn't for the show and I'm delighted that it has helped me to find a wider audience.

There's a fantastic camaraderie among comedians on the stand-up circuit – we're literally all in it together. So another thing I was genuinely scared about was being judged by my peers for doing the show. I was worried that they might think less of me for 'selling out'. We all wear the slog of the comedy circuit like a badge of honour. From the periphery, hands pressed up against the glass, prime-time TV looks like a walk in the park by comparison. This bothered me so much that I didn't even mention to my mates on the circuit that I'd auditioned for the programme until my episode had aired on television. *Surprise!* In hindsight, I was being a complete idiot. The comedy circuit has been nothing but supportive of me since my first gig, and I was blown away by all the kind words and messages I received from other comedians after they had seen me on the show. I really should have known better than to doubt them, myself or the great British public.

Of course, the main reason I decided to audition for *Britain's Got Talent* was to meet Ant and Dec. I think this is something most Geordies want to achieve at some point in their lives. But I also did it because I thought it would help me develop as a performer. Which sounds as though I take myself very seriously indeed. The fact is, a lot of my comedy idols have stepped out on to that stage at the Hammersmith Apollo, so I thought it would be nice (okay, bloody brilliant) to follow in their footsteps.

I still can't believe I made it there at all, and even now I can't quite get my head around what happened next. This comedy thing was only meant to be a laugh. At most it was supposed to be a hobby, something I did in my spare time while holding down a sensible job at Sunderland City Council. I never for a moment expected it to take over my life. But I'm bloody delighted that it has.

ORDEAL BY COWELL

I remember my audition at the Lowry in Salford very clearly. A lot of filming takes place for the *Britain's Got Talent* audition shows, so it was a long day of answering questions on camera, getting some back-story footage.

'Why are you auditioning for *Britain's Got Talent?*'
Good question. I wish I could answer that.
'Are you confident about your performance?'

Well, I was until you asked that question and made me doubt myself.

'Do you think your family are proud of you?'

I should fucking hope so!

So, by the time I got onstage, my fingers already had blisters from all the typing I'd been doing. But one good thing about being kept busy all day was that my nerves didn't have the chance to kick in until the very last second. I'd been building up to that moment all day and suddenly I was standing with Ant and Dec in the wings and it was time. As I walked out onstage I don't know what I was more scared about – Simon Cowell's reputation for speaking the blunt truth or just the mere fact of two thousand pairs of eyes all focused on me.

Of course, Simon threw me a curve ball straight away by asking a question I hadn't prepared an answer for. I honestly believed I'd thought of everything the judges might ask me. Obviously not. Simon asked me how long I hadn't been able to speak and I didn't have an answer – there is a deep irony in that. Thankfully, having considered the horrible possibility of standing there with nothing to say, I had at least programmed in 'I just knew you were going to ask me something I hadn't prepared an answer for. Give me a minute while I type out my reply.' My forward thinking had spared me a very awkward moment, but it was still an incredibly stressful way to start my audition.

I began to type in a proper answer, everyone waiting, everyone looking. You know what it's like when everyone's waiting for you to do something – watching as you reverse-park the car, say. And it's a big space. It's something you can do with no problem at all, usually, and yet it takes you four attempts – mounting the kerb, dinging a bumper – as soon as anyone's watching. When people are watching you do something with your hands, the nerves kick in. The last thing I needed right then was to be all fingers and thumbs and for some nonsense to come spilling out.

After that baptism of fire, everything went to plan. My worries about the audience not getting my material disappeared. In fact, I knew I was off to a good start even before I'd said a word because people were howling with laughter at the slogan on my T-shirt – I'd worn my blue 'I'm Only In It For The Parking' one. I knew that would get a big reaction. I could hear the audience, but I couldn't see much because of the stage lights (even the judges were quite hard to make out). But the vibe I felt from the auditorium was really positive. The atmosphere was electric – a cliché but completely accurate – and the laughter was incredibly loud. Exactly what I'd hoped for and dreamed of. I knew that if I could just keep up this level of energy I'd have done the best I possibly could. And, without wanting to sound too much like my mam, that's all you can ask of yourself.

They loved the first joke and continued to lap up each punchline with roars of laughter. I'd never had an audience that big before. The sound it makes is incredible and it feeds you. One of the most memorable moments was hearing Amanda Holden absolutely cackle at one of my gags – I've never heard a noise quite like it in my life. As my set finished, the judges got up to give me a standing ovation and the rest of the audience quickly followed suit. It was one of the most amazing moments I've ever experienced onstage.

I wish I could remember what the judges said to me after my performance. I know it was very complimentary, but the whole thing is such a blur. I can still remember the buzz, though. It was similar to the feeling I had after my first ever gig in Sunderland. As I walked offstage and was met by a jubilant Ant and Dec, my only wish was that I could go back five minutes later and do it all over again. Throughout my *Britain's Got Talent* experience, I kept thinking back to that amazing first audition and it made me hungry to experience the feeling again.

If anyone who hasn't already seen it would like to, my audition is on YouTube. I think whoever uploaded it is taking the piss, though, because the comments are disabled.

I would have to wait a few months to realize what an impact my *Britain's Got Talent* audition would have. It was recorded in February but wasn't televised until May. I was gigging in London on the Saturday night it was shown on ITV, so I didn't get to watch it until the next day. I knew the exact moment when I had been on, though, because my phone notifications went crazy. I was getting messages from what seemed like everyone I had ever known and plenty of people I didn't. Best of all, Timmy Mallett started to follow me on Twitter. My phone drowned in notifications for the next two weeks or so. It was all getting a bit too much to handle.

Most people on social media were thrilled for me, saying how funny I was and wishing me all the best for the next round, the semi-final. Thanks very much! The outpouring of goodwill was really breathtaking. But not everyone on the internet was on my side. That's to be expected, really. There's always some keyboard warrior hiding behind a screen trying to burst your bubble. Many of the comments were simply variations of 'You're not funny', which is fine. I don't mind that at all. My comedy isn't going to be everyone's bag and I'm okay with that. If everybody in the world found me funny, I'd suggest I was doing comedy wrong.

The thing about comedy is that it's always very subjective, but that's what makes it so exciting. Whatever your sense of humour, you're going to find something you'll like, and I wouldn't have it any other way. That's what comedy is. But maybe you can find a better use of your time than telling people on Twitter that you have a different sense of humour from them. Is there a hole in your life? Maybe it's time to try a new hobby.

Other comments were the usual bollocks about getting the sympathy vote. I can't help it if I'm disabled *and* talented.

PUSHING MY BUTTONS

What got to me most were the comments that implied I was pressing a button onstage and someone else was doing all the hard work, such as writing the jokes. For fuck's sake. I find it very insulting that some people think I can't possibly be capable of being funny on my own because I'm a disabled bloke. For a start, if anyone else thought up some of the stuff I do, they certainly wouldn't get away with it. Most of my jokes are about me and my life experiences, so it would be virtually impossible for someone else to write them for me.

My act isn't about pressing a few buttons onstage and that's the job done. It's much more complicated than that. Like every comedian, not only do I have to read the audience and decide which jokes are going to work best on this particular bunch of people, I also *perform* onstage. I may not be able to talk, but my comedy is as much about my facial expressions, mannerisms and gestures as it is about the writing. One won't work without the other.

Several people even thought I just 'played a tape' while onstage! Well, this isn't 1986, cassette tapes are no longer a thing and I'm not some shit boy band miming away on *Top of the Pops*.

After a while, those comments started to get to me. Here I was working my arse off to try to be as successful as possible, but those people didn't want to give me any credit at all. I decided to try to ignore the negative stuff, but that's easier said than done. All it takes is one glance at one phone notification from Twitter letting me know that I've got a tweet about how I'm not funny in the slightest and all of a sudden I'm logging on and reading the whole thread, trying to figure out why these people feel the need to tell me that.

In some cases it's obvious: they get a kick out of trolling, and they don't matter to me. It's the ones who seem more intelligent who bother me the most. Those people should know better. Even when you try to reason with them by talking to them directly, you still can't get very far. It's probably a waste of time trying. We seem to be living in an age where someone is either right or wrong: there's no room for compromise. 'If you don't agree with me, you must be an idiot.' It's very hard to have a conversation with somebody who thinks in black and white like that.

On the upside, I do enjoy trolling the trolls. Social media has given keyboard warriors a forum to go wild without anyone pulling them up on it. That's why I always try to reason with these people and make an effort to see where they're coming from. More often than not, I'll find they have no real basis for their comments – maybe they've heard it elsewhere and are parroting it. I take great pleasure in winding them up when they're trying to do the same to me. It's similar to dealing with a heckle in a comedy club (or how I imagine that to be, given that no one's yet stepped up to try me; there's a challenge for you). And I could do it all day long. So, if you want to troll me then bring it on, but don't be surprised if I make you look like an idiot to the rest of the world.

So, anyway, there I was in June 2018, standing on the stage at the Hammersmith Apollo in the final. I'd chewed it over, pros and cons, but in the end I'd cancelled my summer holiday to be there (non-refundable deposit, let me add) because it clashed. Good decision, Lee.

A million and one things were racing through my mind:

- How the fuck did this happen?
- Well, this is a big crowd
- I'm sure this was only supposed to be a hobby
- Does my T-shirt look good on TV?
- Do I look good on TV?
- Did I lock my door when I left home this morning?
- Is my grandma watching at home?
- Is *anyone* watching at home?
- Will I even be allowed home if I don't win?
- No, seriously, how the fuck did I get here?
- Oh, Christ, Dec is talking to me, I'd better pay attention . . .

By the grand old age of thirty-seven, I'd had quite a few brilliant moments. I'd seen the sunset in Ibiza with my best mates, I'd graduated from university with a master's, and I'd watched Newcastle United beat Sunderland 5–0 at St James' Park. But the reason my *Britain's Got Talent* victory topped all of these was because it was the fulfilment of a dream that had seemed impossible.

The whole experience was amazing from start to finish. It was so much fun appearing on the show, and it was great to perform in front of such a huge audience. I made some really good friends along the way, and the reaction from the general public was phenomenal. I never expected to do as well as I did.

So, what happened next? Obviously I'm a lot richer now. Please don't tell the Department of Work and Pensions. I really need those benefits. But, seriously, winning the show has changed my life in so many ways. I'm busier than I ever was before as a comedian. I've had my first nationwide tour, and the opportunity to write this book. Thanks for buying it. I've written it all myself. It's nearly killed me. You're welcome. People have been so supportive. I'm always getting stopped for selfies and being congratulated. It takes twice as long to get anywhere, these days, but it's all been really brilliant. I'm very grateful.

But the simple fact that people are engaging with me a lot more than they've ever done before is one of the best things to come out of *Britain's Got Talent*. For the first time, people seem comfortable talking to me, as a disabled person, right from the off. I'm so used to being stared at for negative reasons that it's wonderful, if a little unnerving at times, to be stared at for positive ones.

I'm used to having people look at me weirdly when they first see me, perhaps doing a double-take, then just walking past without so much as a hello. And, to be honest, that kind of reaction made me feel like shit. Like I was somehow inferior to everyone else just because I was different. I used to avoid walking past large groups of people (teenagers can be the worst at giggling and making comments), just so I didn't have to experience those feelings again and again. Even if this meant walking the long way around, I thought it was better than being stared at. If you've no idea how that feels, you're very lucky indeed.

But now that people are more used to me and my disability, this doesn't happen. And whereas before I might have been shy about having a conversation with someone new, I'm now starting to encourage people to speak to me and will even initiate the conversation.

I've come a long way from that shy eighteen-year-old who had just started university and found himself for the first time outside the protective barrier of his family. It's just a shame that I've had to appear on a television show to be able to get to this point of relative social normality – not something most disabled people get the opportunity to do. Being disabled can be a really isolating experience, so it's important that people with disabilities get to socialize as much as possible. That will only happen if they're treated like everyone else.

When I started out in stand-up comedy, I did it because I enjoyed it. I certainly wasn't aiming to spread a positive message about disability. But now I realize that I've been doing this inadvertently every time I step on to a stage. It wasn't my intention, but if it makes people think about the issues surrounding disability, that must be a good thing. Long may it continue.

Winning *Britain's Got Talent* was the final bit of validation I needed to prove to myself that I could be a successful comedian despite everything life had thrown at me. When Dec said those magical words in the final – 'The winner of *Britain's Got Talent* 2018 is . . . Lost Voice Guy!' – *that* was the moment when I discovered that it's possible to make your dreams a reality, if you have the nerve and really want them, and are lucky enough to have people who love you backing you up all the way.

BEWARE OF FAITH HEALERS IN CONSETT

At this point, in best *BGT* tradition, I'm going to introduce my grandma. I've mentioned my nana and grandad on my mam's side a fair bit, but not so much my grandma and grandad on my dad's side. Time I redressed that balance.

I think my grandma was more pleased than anyone when I won *Britain's Got Talent*. In fact, she was almost on the telly as much as I was during the final. I'm sure she chose that particular seat in the audience on purpose because she knew she'd be getting some of the limelight. And the way she hugged Simon Cowell at the end when all my family got up onstage after I'd won, well, I thought she was never going to let him go. Honestly, I feared for his safety.

My grandma tells everyone she sees that Lost Voice Guy is her grandson. Literally everybody! I've had people come up to me after my shows telling me they've met my grandma and how lovely she is. If I ever get enough time off to go on another holiday, I won't be surprised if I'm accosted on a remote beach in Greece by people my grandma's been telling about me.

I'm glad she's proud of me. Grandad, too. It means a lot because, whether I could help it or not, I've put them through a lot by being disabled. I know they love me regardless but it's still nice to be able to put a smile on their faces when I can.

My grandma has always had the best intentions for me . . . even though it hasn't always seemed that way. The thing is, she's very religious so when I was younger she took me to a faith healer in a church in Consett to see if I could be cured. It should have been obvious that the whole faith-healer thing was a bad idea. If this guy really had a direct link to a higher power, why would he have chosen to live in Consett? Then again, I guess there's no shortage of people there who need healing . . . As it happened, I developed epilepsy a few months after the visit, so as far as his application for divine intervention could be seen to have had any impact on my situation, it actually made it considerably worse. I didn't sue him, though. I was very compassionate like that, as a fourteen-year-old. Plus I had enough on my plate dealing with the epilepsy, without wondering what I was going to wear for my big day in court. Besides, my grandma wouldn't have liked it.

But, joking aside, this was just another example of my grandma and grandad wanting the best for me. And even if the miracle cure couldn't be effected, at least I got ten minutes' worth of material out of it.

'How does it feel to be an inspiration?'

I've got quite a lot to say about this.

Over the years, I don't think I've ever felt like much of an inspiration. I'm just a disabled bloke trying to get on with his life and have a laugh along the way. There are plenty of other amazing people who are doing far more inspirational things than I am. I know people who have climbed mountains and run marathons for charity, given up their free time to help out others who are less fortunate than them.

Then there are the doctors and nurses who work for the NHS with little reward or credit. They are the individuals I find inspiring and I've done nothing in comparison to them (although having to put up with Simon Cowell probably earns me a 'well done' sticker). Standing onstage for an hour a few times a week isn't *that* hard work, so I don't see it as being worthy of such high praise.

On the other hand, no one can deny that a tendency to undervalue ourselves tends to go with the territory, where being disabled is concerned. What we see in the eyes of able-bodied fellow citizens isn't always conducive to high self-esteem. The only time disabled people can rely on feeling like they're at the heart of the nation's culture and truly valued by the society around them is once every four years when everyone watches the Paralympics for a couple of weeks. In terms of the British public in general and their relationship with disability, this feels a bit like having an affair. It's enjoyable while it lasts, and it makes people feel better about themselves, but in the end they don't want to commit to anything long-term so they step away with some fond memories and try to go back to life as it was before.

It might not be the done thing for a disabled person to have a bit of a moan about the Paralympics, but that's not going to stop me. Here goes.

Part of the problem is that the adverts make all disabled people look amazingly talented. It's a sorry state of affairs when even a major national television channel seems to be joining the long queue of people lining up to take the piss out of you for not being that über-person. There's nothing I like better than being reminded that I'm not even one of the best disabled people around. I'm distinctly average at most, and I'm receiving the message loud and clear. But just imagine what I could have achieved if I was actually a superhuman! I could have won gold medals. I could have had a fancy house in South Africa. I could have murdered my supermodel girlfriend. I could be spending thirteen years in jail right now . . . So thank fuck I'm a lazy bastard with absolutely no talent for sport.

All that said, I've loved what the Paralympics has achieved in recent times, opening people's eyes to a community of others who are often overlooked. Although it made me feel just a tad inadequate, I even enjoyed Channel 4's 'Yes We Can' advert. We've come a long way from people pitying our mere existence. There are some amazing athletes out there, but they can't speak for us all. At the end of the day, I'm not superhuman. I'm just human, like every other disabled person. We're simply here, trying to get by – like everyone else, in fact.

Just because I'm allowed to park closer to Tesco doesn't automatically mean I get to wear the title 'superhuman'. I struggle to wipe my own arse, never mind do anything more demanding. That doesn't sound very super to me.

So, much as I love sport, the Paralympics seems to suggest that the only good disabled people are the successful ones, and that's the problem I have with the way most people view the event. It's inspiration porn of the highest order and I'm not a fan. You can't just put disabled people into two groups – the can-dos and the can't-dos – because it's not as simple as that. It's also a very dangerous game to play as it suggests to the rest of society that some disabled people aren't as worthy of attention and support as others.

The current Conservative government isn't helping matters. It would seem that they have a very weird relationship with disabled people. We are seen either as superhuman or as some sort of burden on society. There just isn't any middle ground. We are encouraged to go out and become Paralympic superstars, with plenty of funding pumped into running, jumping, cycling and swimming, but they deny us the basic human right of living independently.

Here's the big question: is it the case that the only acceptable disabled person is a successful Paralympian? And, if so, how are we expected to become a success of any description when we can't survive financially day to day? I'm becoming more and more convinced that the government is playing a giant disabled version of *The Hunger Games*, devised to root out the 'best' disabled people while the rest of us wither and die. The closure of the Independent Living Fund has already got rid of a few of us.

It isn't our fault that we need a bit more money than non-disabled people to survive. For example, I often have to rely on getting taxis rather than using public transport because it's easier for me to cope with. When I go away, I always have to take someone with me to support me, which usually means booking an extra hotel room. It's the same with tickets for music gigs and theatre shows. All these little things add up over time and become big, expensive things.

I feel like a hypocrite saying all this now that I have my *Britain's Got Talent* dollar in the bank, but I've experienced the hardships first hand as well. The fact is that many disabled people can't make that money, and I'm not sure how taking money away from us is going to help. I'm not going to get better magically just because my benefits have been cut. I'm sick of phoning Downing Street every morning and saying, 'I'm sorry

I've woken up disabled again, Prime Minister. I'll try
harder tomorrow . . .'

I've had first-hand experience of the current Social
Services regime's wilful incompetence, too. About a
year ago, I had to ring up their helpline because I had
some questions about my benefits. The bloke on the
phone refused to speak to me because I couldn't prove
that I was the one typing. I probably didn't help the
situation by pointing out that he couldn't prove it was
him speaking, either. But when you think about it, he
could have been anyone. I couldn't see him, and he
couldn't see me, because that's how telephones fucking
work.

The government has a responsibility here. They can't
just champion our successes and ignore us when we
need help. Now is not the time to cut benefits and put
lives at risk. If the Paralympics have taught us anything,
it's that disabled people aren't all scroungers and
benefits cheats. The general public needs to see that
disabled people can contribute an awful lot to society
all of the time, not just for a couple of weeks every four
years at a sporting event.

What I want to say to people is, 'Please don't pity me,
don't feel sorry for me.' In the grand scheme of things,
I'm not some paragon of virtue who struggles
heroically to play the tricky cards Destiny has dealt
him. Okay, well, maybe on my best days I am. But on
my worst days I can be a bit of a dickhead. I take
do-gooders prisoner. That's not a figure of speech, it's
something I actually did.

A few years ago – back when I had a proper job – I was walking home from work when a bloke tried to help me cross the road. Because obviously I'm incapable of turning my head to the right and then to the left and moving forwards or not accordingly. I tried to indicate to him that I was fine on my own, thanks, but he was insistent. So I decided to let him get on with it. He took my hand and walked me across the road. That was when the fun started. Instead of letting go of his hand on the other side, I decided it would be more entertaining to keep hold of it. In fact, I kept hold of it all the way home. That was a fifteen-minute walk. Obviously, I went the long way home, just to drag it out a bit. I went through the park and up the high street. Every time he tried to let go, I would wobble to make him panic. I can see that from the outside this might look a little harsh on my part – basically I had taken the bloke prisoner just for assuming something he shouldn't have. But when you've been in as many situations as I have (and probably a lot of other disabled people have experienced the same thing) when supposedly well-meaning people take away the little bit of independence that you do have and don't listen when you try to stop them, sometimes you just feel like evening the score.

That's why playing with people's misconceptions of me is one of my favourite things to do. I'm the sort of guy who presses every button in the lift, just as I'm getting out of it. I'm the kind of guy who makes people move out of the disabled space on the train, even when the whole carriage is empty. I'm that person who gets up to do karaoke, then pretends the microphone is broken when no sound comes out of my mouth.

Even after all this bad behaviour, people come up to me and tell me what an inspiration I am to them. They say how brave I am to get up on stage. But I don't see myself as being here to inspire others and, in all honesty, I'm tired of being called an inspiration. Don't be mistaken. I'm inspired by disabled people all the time, but not just because they're disabled.

Inspirational quotes are everywhere these days, which just makes it worse for people like me. I can guarantee that at least a couple of your friends have them plastered all over their walls at home. They probably say things like 'Fill a house with love, and it becomes a home' or maybe 'We create our tomorrow by what we dream today.' But whether you're looking to trite aphorisms or to the disabled for your inspiration, you're barking up the wrong tree.

The inspirational quotes that really get to me are shared on Facebook, quotes like 'The only disability in life is a bad attitude.' Fuck off. I don't get out of bed in the morning to make other people feel better about their lives. And if that makes me a monster, then so be it.

Being nice to the stairs in my flat hasn't turned them into a ramp yet. And no amount of positive thinking is going to help that blind man when he walks into a bookshop.

Right, now we've got that out in the open, let's press on.

THE *ROYAL VARIETY* IS THE SPICE OF LIFE

10

grew up watching *Live at the Apollo* on the TV. I hardly missed an episode because it was the only game in town for people who wanted to see the best comedians in the world but couldn't be arsed to go to a venue (or couldn't afford it, maybe because their benefits have been slashed). Like performing at the Comedy Store, it's something that almost every comic aspires to do at some point in their career.

When I first started doing comedy, my mates used to joke that one day they'd see me on the show. None of us ever really thought it would happen, especially me. I thought I'd never be good enough. There are hundreds (maybe thousands – everyone's a fucking joker, these days) of very talented comedians all over the country and only a handful have had the honour of walking through that *Live at the Apollo* sign – all those little light-bulbs blinding you and making you sweat even more – and on to that stage.

Fast-forward to 2018, and it was me. There I was filming my *Live at the Apollo* set in front of a great Hammersmith Apollo audience, which included my parents and my best mates. Strangely enough, I was more nervous about that gig than I've ever been for anything else – even the final of *Britain's Got Talent*. I was so nervous I can't really remember what happened that night, it remained a blur until I was able to watch it broadcast on BBC Two a few months later. I made sure I savoured every second of it.

Life sometimes offers you moments like that. And they're amazing. You feel like you're flying. Life is great. You are fucking fantastic. Nothing and no one can touch you. But however many wonderful moments I've had, there are also those other moments that are a bit shit and bring you right back down to earth. These are some of my favourite low points so far:

Getting upstaged by grass. I was doing a gig at Doncaster football stadium and my dressing room was actually one of the directors' boxes that looked out on to the pitch. A woman came in asking if it was okay for her to get a photo. 'Yes, of course!' I said, as I got my photo face ready. No mean feat. She walked right past me and took a photo of the pitch. Wounded.

Getting shown to the wrong dressing room. It was around Christmas and I was due to perform at a gig in Camden in London. I got a bit lost on the way to the venue, started to get very stressed, and ended up asking for directions from a bouncer. He took me to the place, then said he'd guide me to the green room. Very helpful, I thought. He took me through a crowd of young people who were dancing and enjoying a Christmas night out. This is strange, I thought. This didn't look like a comedy club at all, but I trusted that the bouncer knew what he was doing. I certainly didn't. It was only when I finally entered the green room that I realized there had been a massive mix-up. I came face to face with a band who were getting ready to go on stage. I wasn't at the comedy club. I was at a music venue called Dingwalls. Fuck knows what the bouncer thought I was going to sing. Maybe Simon and Garfunkel's 'The Sound of Silence'.

Being mistaken for Lee Nelson. I have the BBC Radio 2 reception to thank for this one. I was there to appear on *The Steve Wright Show* to talk about my sitcom *Ability*. Somehow my guest pass had 'Lee Nelson' written on it instead of 'Lee Ridley'. No offence to the other Lee, but we're hardly similar acts. And 'chav' isn't an option on my talker.

Not even being able to have a shit in peace. Of all the hotels this could have happened at, it had to happen at the poshest: the Grosvenor House Hotel in London. It had been a long day and I was settling down in my room for the night. As a part of this, as with most people, ablutions were involved. I decided to go to the toilet. I didn't think I was going to be disturbed that night so I didn't bother to close the bathroom door. It was only when I was mid-shit that I realized I'd made a big error. Because it was then that a chambermaid decided to knock on the door and ask if I wanted my bed turned down. If you're like me and have no idea what that means, it's when the maid turns the covers of the bed down so you can just slip in at night . . . If you're lucky they leave a little chocolate as well. Until that point in life, I didn't even know that this was a thing. Anyway, as I wasn't expecting anyone this whole situation took me by surprise. To say the least. I thought that if I just kept quiet – something I do effortlessly – she'd go away. But she didn't. Instead, she decided to let herself into the room while I was still on the toilet with the bathroom door wide open. What made matters worse was that the door to the room was directly opposite the bathroom. That's right, the first thing the chambermaid saw when she came in was me trying to take a dump. She let out a scream and closed the door almost instantly. It was too late, though. The damage had been done. That's an image she's never going to get out of her head.

The taxi driver who wouldn't let me sit in the front. I'm using this particular incident as an example but I could easily have chosen from about ten other stories of various taxi drivers acting like dickheads towards me. Most of the time they simply don't know how to treat a disabled person and don't mean to be rude. That leaves one or two who definitely need some equality and diversity training. On this occasion I had attempted to get into the front seat of the taxi as I always do. It's just easier to get in and out and there's more room. That driver wasn't having any of it. Apparently I couldn't sit in the front for health and safety reasons. He insisted that disabled people had to sit in the back. I asked him to explain his reasoning several times but I never did get a straight answer. After about five minutes of arguing on the side of the road, I sat in the front anyway (as I've mentioned, I'm an awkward bastard). He was still pissed off that I didn't get into the back. He argued his case for the rest of the trip but never once made a bit of sense. That was a really long and awkward half-hour journey. I'd like to give a special shout-out to all the taxi drivers who lose their shit when I get into the car, then ask if I'm travelling alone or if my friend is coming with me too. What fucking difference does it make where I sit in the car or who's coming with me?

My chocolate cake train horror. Let me explain to you what the splash zone is. It's the area in front of me where you should *never* sit when I'm eating. Sea World have a splash zone for when their whales get the audience wet. This is a similar thing but involving food instead of water. So, while Sea World's splash zone is fun, mine is not. Most of my friends know to stay out of the splash zone at all costs. Entering the zone puts you at extreme danger – especially if I'm eating Coco Pops and you value your eyesight. The problem is that not everyone can stay out of the splash zone all of the time. This is especially the case on train journeys when I've been lucky enough to get a table seat and I'm sitting opposite someone. Those tables are shallow. Unless you're already intimate with someone and love them dearly, it's never a great idea to be opposite someone who's eating on a train. More often than not, I won't eat if a random person is facing me. They have no idea that the splash zone exists, and I'd rather starve to death than give them a first-hand experience of it. Sadly, this can't always be the case. For health reasons, I have no other option sometimes than to eat on the train.

It was on one of these occasions that the splash zone caused me untold amounts of embarrassment. I was sitting in the first-class carriage on the train, eating a nice piece of chocolate cake, when some posh bloke came and sat opposite me. His suit was freshly pressed and his shoes were shiny. In hindsight, I should have taken this pristine outfit as a warning to cut my losses and stop eating immediately. But it was *really* nice cake. Everything went fine for a while. And then I got lured into a false sense of security. I thought I was going to get away with eating in close proximity to a stranger without incident. Then I felt it coming. It wasn't bad at first, but I knew I definitely needed to cough. And I knew what sort of result that would bring if I allowed it to happen. I tried to keep it in but that just made the situation worse. The more I tried to suppress my cough, the more it fought to come out. After a few minutes of battling, I lost the fight. The cough exited at full speed with the obvious result that some of my chocolate cake came with it and covered the well-dressed man. I was so embarrassed. I tried to apologize and he said it was fine, but I could tell that it wasn't. His face said it all. I had to avoid eye contact with him for the rest of the journey. That was a very long three hours.

Accidentally playing porn on my talker at work. I didn't intentionally play a porn clip while I was in a meeting at work at the council. It just sort of happened. Honest, guv. The problem arose because I use the same talker for my day-to-day conversations and for when I'm making jokes onstage. One particular piece of joke material involves me trying to find some music to play but instead playing, by accident, a clip of a woman enjoying herself at volume, which is taken from a porn movie. This is usually hilarious when I do it onstage. It wasn't as hilarious when I accidentally played it at a work meeting in front of my colleagues and the director of communications of Sunderland council. I don't even know how I managed to do it, but I did. I was horrified. I did try explaining that it was part of my set. I don't think anyone believed me.

The woman in the post office who insisted on writing every-thing down. This kind of thing happens more than I would like. Every once in a while I'll meet someone who thinks I'm deaf as well as speechless and writes everything down instead of speaking to me. It's a consequence of not being used to dealing with disabled people. That doesn't make it any less frustrating. As I've explained, I'm typically British so I don't like making a fuss (unless a taxi driver has royally pissed me off: special dispensation for irritating taxi drivers). So instead of correcting her and letting her know that I can actually hear perfectly fine, I just let her get on with it. The conversation took a very long time indeed. And in the end I couldn't understand her writing anyway. Admittedly all this was partly my fault for not being brave enough to tell her that she was doing something wrong.

Reality checks that bring me back down to earth with a bump aside, recently life's been amazing experience after amazing experience that I couldn't have dreamed of having. For example, here's one question I never imagined needing to ask myself: 'So, what *does* one wear to the *Royal Variety Performance?*'

TUXEDO T-SHIRTS AND OTHER FASHION NOTES

It may surprise you to hear this, but my wardrobe is not littered with clothes suitable for a royal occasion. Before the event, the poshest outfit I owned was the suit I'd worn for my sister's wedding a few years back, and that just wasn't going to be good enough. For a start, I'm a bit fatter (okay, a lot fatter) than I was back then. Don't blame me, blame Pâtisserie Valerie. The only way I could possibly wear that suit was if I held my breath for the whole day, which was not an option, unless I was prepared to collapse and die in front of the Royal Family. It would have made the show more memorable for them, but wouldn't have been so great for Mam and Dad.

I think my mam was secretly pleased that I needed a new outfit because it meant she could help me choose something. And when I say 'help me', I mean she bought me something to wear and demanded I wear it. She wanted me to look my best for the royals and, for once, I didn't mind her taking over. I did get to have some say. I knew I couldn't get away with one of my usual slogan T-shirts. But I did want to wear something that was in keeping with my style – Meghan and I have such a lot in common in that sense. We decided I'd wear a T-shirt with a tuxedo printed on it. I wouldn't usually present myself as a fashion leader but I think it was the right choice.

My head is still fried by what was a totally surreal experience. Best described as being like stepping through your television screen into a parallel universe, the whole day was just unbelievable. From arriving at the stage door of the Palladium and having to sign autographs for loads of fans – believe it or not, some of them were there for me – to actually getting to shake Prince Harry's hand . . . It's time to use the J-word. What a journey it's been.

When it came to the day of the *Royal Variety Performance*, I woke up as early as a small child on Christmas morning. The excitement was just too much. You think you'll get used to it after a while – 'Oh, it's *The One Show* sofa,' or 'Oh, it's Phillip Schofield.' But just as you start to take things in your stride, something happens that ups the ante. That feeling of excitement ahead of the *Royal Variety Performance* was so, well, *exciting*. But the early start also meant that I had more time to get nervous. It's not every day that you get to perform in front of royalty. It felt like a really big deal. What if they didn't find me funny? What if I hit the wrong button and ended up swearing at Prince Harry?

The very nice lady looking after me for the day did a good job. I mostly remember her because she kept telling me to take my time and watch my step. Not just once or twice. She seemed to constantly want me to take my time and watch my step. Over and over again, I'm telling you. It would have been annoying if she hadn't been such a sweet woman. In other circumstances I'd have led her around the houses, punishing her for patronizing me. But I was in the mood to find it all very amusing.

I was given the dressing room closest to the stage to make it easier for me. Apparently it was the same dressing room that Kylie Minogue had used the week before. Sometimes, when perks like that are up for grabs, it's almost worth being disabled. First things first. I checked under the sofa to see if she had left anything behind that I could sell on eBay. No luck. But it was a very nice dressing room (I doubt Kylie would put up with some of the poor excuses for green rooms that I've had the pleasure of gracing over the years). And it was made even nicer by the fact that the production team had left a load of cakes in the fridge. But I couldn't eat them. I couldn't risk busting out of my new trousers onstage, hitting Meghan in the eye with a rogue button, and treating her to the sight of my underpants as my trousers slid down around my ankles.

During rehearsals all the performers were ushered to the backstage area to get ready to practise the closing number of the night – Take That were going to do a version of 'Never Forget', a rock-solid karaoke classic. We were all to come onstage for this bit. I just hoped they didn't want me to sing along.

Imposter syndrome kicked in. I had visions of being found out and escorted off the premises by security! 'You in the ridiculous T-shirt, what are you doing here? I said, what are you doing here? Speak up, man!' At the end of the song, we all had to clap along – imagine Queen's 'We Will Rock You' (or maybe even Take That's 'Never Forget') but on acid. We must have rehearsed it three or four times, but even with the director standing in front of us and showing us exactly what to do, I had little idea what I was supposed to be doing, other than grinning madly. I don't really have any sense of rhythm to start with, so I had no chance of doing it in time with everyone else anyway. I knew I'd just have to wing it and hope for the best.

The rehearsal of the royal line-up was next. Let me tell you, nothing is left to chance. It's a military operation. This would be the part of the night where we'd get introduced to Prince Harry and Meghan. We were told we had to address Prince Harry as 'Your Royal Highness' and Meghan as 'ma'am'. My talker nailed the pronunciation of 'Your Royal Highness', so I had no problems there. It was a very different story when it came to saying 'ma'am'. My talker didn't like the word 'ma'am' at all and kept pronouncing it as 'Mam' instead. That's a whole different kettle of fish. And, although Meghan and my mother are both beautiful women, I couldn't very well be saying, 'Pleased to meet you, Mam,' to Meghan. She would have thought I was crazy, downright rude or that I wanted to be adopted.

I went back to my dressing room and got to work on fixing the problem. This was not the time for a talker malfunction.

By the time they were ready for me to rehearse my set I had already changed into the second of four tuxedo T-shirts (I always carry spare tops because I'm such a mucky pup!). As it was the first time I was standing on the Palladium stage alone, without having to elbow Gary Barlow or George Ezra out of the way, I was able to take in the view a bit more. The Palladium is a beautiful venue with such a rich history. So many great performers had been exactly where I was standing. The thought gave me goosebumps. It was at this point that it suddenly struck me where I was and what I was doing. You might expect some mild expletives, but for a few moments I could only think, Wow! It was an 'I can fly' moment that I wanted to last for ever, to soak up and imprint on my mind. Then I was interrupted by a techie who wanted to do a soundcheck.

Rehearsing a comedy set in an empty venue is always a bizarre thing to do. I was performing to nobody as I ran through my jokes for the night. Even the sound guy wasn't listening any more. It's a bit pointless. It's not as if I'm going to mess up my lines. Thankfully, my dad and mam (my real one, not Meghan, who was now most definitely 'ma'am') were watching in the auditorium and politely laughing in all the right places, like good parents do, or I would have been performing to a rather unnerving silence.

And that was that. All the rehearsing had been done and it was almost time for the main event. I went back to my dressing room to wait my turn. I'll admit that I did manage to sneak a bit of cake down my throat. Thank God for T-shirt number three. And, in the end, who would care if the button on my trousers popped off? I needed the sugar rush to help me deal with the jangling nerves.

As the show got under way, I tried to watch the other performers on the television in Kylie's dressing room but, to be honest, I didn't really take much of it in. It looked like a fantastic show but I was too nervous to concentrate. In fact, I was too nervous to do most things . . . including going to the toilet for a pre-show pee. Note to self: always go for a pre-show pee.

Eventually, the lovely take-your-time-and-watch-your-step lady came back to escort me to the stage for my performance. Only this time I took a lot more notice of her wise words and did actually take my time and watch my step. This wasn't the moment to be falling down and cracking my head open. Despite the company, all the Queen's horses and all the Queen's men couldn't have put me back together again in time to do my set.

Simon Cowell was there, especially to introduce me on stage, which was a really lovely thing to do and meant a lot to me. I was walked on to the stage by my glamorous assistant – doesn't everyone have one of those? In fact, I don't always have someone walk me on to the stage: I just knew some jobsworth from the Department of Work and Pensions would be watching at home so I wanted to leave them in no doubt of my entitlement. I think I did a good job.

And my set wasn't bad either. I was very pleased with the reaction that night: everyone seemed to really enjoy it and buy into every punch-line, which is all you can ask for as a comedian (although I might add cake to my rider). I did keep slyly looking up at the royal box to see if His Royal Highness and Ma'am were loving it as much as the rest of the audience. Turns out it's quite pleasing to get a royal seal of approval.

The performance was all over in the blink of an eye. The tricky part was still to come, though. I'd been told I had to bow twice. Once to the audience and once to the royal box. You'll know by now that I'm quite unsteady on my feet at the best of times. But in this instance there were no concessions for the disabled. The last thing I wanted to do was lose my balance and topple over after I'd already done the hard work. (Although better to fall flat on my face *after* the hard work than before, I suppose.) Imagine the embarrassment. I'd have to rewrite my moments-that-bring-you-down-to-earth list, for a start. And the take-your-time-and-watch-your-step lady would have been very disappointed in me. I bowed tentatively to the audience and managed to stay upright. Then, as directed, I turned to the royals and bowed again. I was still standing after that, too. It was a Christmas miracle.

I could relax for a while, but not for long. I still had the Take That finale to participate in. Needless to say, I didn't remember what I had to do during the song. To be fair, I don't think many of the acts did. We all just stood there clapping randomly and hoping it was in the right place – but who cared? It was an amazing moment to be a part of. I was onstage with Take That, 'singing' 'Never Forget', which is pretty damn memorable.

After that awkward moment on *Britain's Got Talent* when Simon asked me a question I didn't have a ready answer for, I was more prepared this time. I knew the royals might ask me something so I had thought of some replies to store in my talker just in case. Stuff like 'Yes, I've really enjoyed myself' and 'Thank you, I'm glad you enjoyed it.' The sort of charm-offensive that makes people ask to sit next to you at dinner. My favourite pre-emptive reply was 'Fancy seeing you here!' But in the end I didn't have the guts to use it.

As it turns out, I didn't use any of my pre-programmed replies. Call me crazy, but I decided to go with the flow instead. When Meghan asked me something (protocol dictates that I can't possibly tell you what: I'd have to kill you), I just typed out my answer on the spot. She seemed happy to wait – imagine if she had stood there rolling her eyes or tapping an impatient foot – so I didn't feel under any pressure to rush. She also told me that Harry had been looking forward to seeing my act, which blew my mind. I've never thought about the likes of the Queen watching me on the television in her dressing-gown and slippers. That's an image to conjure with. But what I'm most curious about is the inappropriate remark Prince Philip allegedly made about me when he saw me on his screen. I'm sure it was something very politically incorrect. And I'm sure I would have found it really funny.

When Prince Harry was introduced to me he, too, seemed comfortable enough to allow me to type out my answer and wait for my reply. It was a good thing he wasn't in a hurry, because I wasn't expecting him to ask, 'So, what's Simon Cowell really like?' and I didn't have that answer prepared. Eventually I replied, 'He's just a pussycat when you get to know him.' After all, Simon had stayed around to watch my set, and came back to Kylie's dressing room to congratulate me. I could definitely get used to that kind of treatment.

The 'What is Simon Cowell really like?' question is one I often get asked. The truth is that he's a really lovely bloke (at least, he always has been to me, and that's all you can really go on, isn't it?) . . . and he hasn't paid me to say that. I was a bit scared of him before I actually met him. I had visions of him telling me I wasn't remotely funny in front of the entire nation. It can be hard to come back from that kind of put-down. Thankfully, that didn't happen and instead I had the chance to get to know him better. He's been so supportive, giving me advice and opportunities to perform all over the world at some really special events. I've even had the chance to do some shows in America. It was such a great experience flying first class to Los Angeles – I was speechless on the plane. But that's the problem with being put into flight mode.

COLE'S FROM NEWCASTLE

Simon Cowell was also kind enough to invite me to his summer party in 2018. Even by *Royal Variety* standards that was pretty surreal. All of a sudden I'd gone from hanging out with my mates in my local pub in Newcastle to hanging out with the likes of Cheryl Cole at a very lavish bash in London. The parties have come thick and fast since. Again, I'm not complaining.

As with all good theatrical productions, the after-show party of the *Royal Variety Performance* was the highlight – a very posh affair with a *Who's Who* of famous people on the guest list. And me. We had just finished a lovely meal (by now I was on T-shirt number four) and were up on the dance-floor having a bit of a boogie when I came face to face with another kind of royalty – *television* royalty this time. Paul from the Chuckle Brothers.

I'd be lying if I said meeting Paul from the Chuckle Brothers wasn't the absolute highlight of my night. Forget about Mark from Take That. Forget about Rick Astley. Forget about Prince Harry. This was a Chuckle Brother. Back in the eighties I used to race home from school looking forward to watching the two of them on the TV, and thirty years later, here I was doing the Macarena (well, I was trying to do the Macarena) with one of them. He'd enjoyed my performance. I'd made him laugh. It was the perfect end to a perfect day.

'Are you okay?'

Whether it's after a fall or a fit, I've groped my way back
to consciousness in response to 'Are you okay?' more
than once too often. Luckily for me, the NHS and I
have always been really good friends. I've lost count of
the number of times I've been in hospital. I'm on
first-name terms with most of the staff at the Royal
Victoria Infirmary in Newcastle. I'm only surprised I
don't have my own bed there yet. Except, of course,
there are no beds . . .

Thankfully, most of my visits have been to A and E,
and nothing more serious. But I've been in A and E
so many times that I'm earning reward points. Five
more visits and I get some morphine. If I make it to
twenty-five, I get to choose which nurse helps me out at
bathtime. I once even ended up in hospital on holiday in
Spain. You haven't experienced awkwardness until
you've had to explain to someone who can't speak
English that you can't talk. That was a *very* long game
of charades.

Rather than having a moan about my tendency to
have accidents or get ill, I'm more inclined to think
about how lucky I've been to have the (mostly) fantastic
NHS to look after me. Fingers crossed the Tories don't

win another election and get to realize their dream of turning the glory of our nation into a malfunctioning branch of Starbucks.

One thing's for sure: disabled people living in other parts of the world don't have it nearly as easy as I did. In certain parts of Africa, for example, they still sometimes kill disabled babies at birth, in the belief that they're evil spirits. There are other places where disabled people are treated as witches and sent away to live in camps together. History has taught us that putting people in camps never ends well . . . I definitely wouldn't have survived in Nazi Germany. In fact, disabled people there were among the first to be exterminated. I can't help feeling that we were quite an easy target. There's no way I could have made it up the stairs to hide in an attic, for example.

To me 'Laughter is the best medicine' sounds like something the Conservatives would say to cut waiting times at A and E units. If anything, the best medicine has to be Calpol. With all of its purple goodness, that stuff could cure anything that was wrong with me when I was a child. Mammy, I've just banged my head. Have some Calpol! Mammy, I've just been stung by a bee. Have some Calpol! Mammy, I've just been run over by a lorry, which then reversed back over me before the driver got out to give me a good kick in the balls, and as I lay writhing a random dog made a beeline and started to gnaw at my face. Have some Calpol! For a while when I was young I thought it might even help with my cerebral palsy.

Of course, Calpol couldn't help with that, and it couldn't cure my pneumonia either, but the NHS did. And as I was lying in that hospital bed desperate to get well so I could get back onstage and start doing my job, I couldn't stop thinking about all the people who've cared for me over the years. Without them I definitely wouldn't be here today, and I couldn't have a section all about my various stays in hospital without listing some of the many accidents I've had over the years.

As will have become painfully clear by now, in every sense of those words, one of the main consequences of my cerebral palsy is that I'm not very good at staying upright. In fact, a much more apt name for me would be Lost Balance Guy as I've spent half my life tripping over and falling to the floor. My problem is that I can't react quickly and put out my hands to stop myself, like most people would.

I'd like to say I've blocked some of the accidents from my memory because they were so horrific, but that's kind of hard to do because my dad always insists on taking photos of all my injuries. Don't worry, he doesn't frame them and put them on the wall or anything weird like that. He just likes to have plenty of evidence in case the government tries to claim I'm not disabled any more and stop my benefits. My dad is a very smart man. So, in no particular order, these are my best bumps and bruises.

The one when I got rescued by firemen. I'll start with a recent event. It wasn't a particularly bad fall: it just sort of amused me. You have to take your laughs where you can. I had just moved into my new flat and was still getting my bearings. Being blind is obviously a very different experience, but you can draw some parallels with the way I negotiate a room. For me, it really helps to know where everything is. Every centimetre matters. Anything that's in the wrong place can be a disaster. Flooring is key.

It was my first day on my own and I was looking forward to a relaxing time, a chance to bask in my new pad. That idea was short-lived as I slipped on the laminate flooring and fell on to my arse. Luckily I wasn't hurt, but there was a much bigger problem to contend with than pain. Once I've fallen over I find it very hard to get up by myself; I usually have to have someone to help pick me up. That isn't always possible. I don't have a carer 24/7 and I like it that way. In my old flat, I had devised a system to get myself up off the floor. I would crawl over to the sofa and use that to hoist myself up. It was a struggle – really quite tiring – but it always worked. So, I thought I would try that method in my new flat as well.

I crawled to the sofa and tried to pull myself up. It was at that moment that I remembered my old flat had had carpets: the essential element to this strategy. On this fancy new laminate flooring – one of the features that had really attracted me to the flat – my feet were slipping all over the place and I had absolutely no control over my legs. I was stuck.

I tried several other methods in the hope of returning myself to a vertical position. These included pulling myself up the stairs so that I'd be at a better angle from which to start the attempt, trying to hoist myself up using the quilt on the bed and, most unhygienic, using the toilet bowl to lift myself off the floor. Alas, none worked. I had to admit defeat, call my mam and ask her to come and rescue me. I thought that would be the end of the matter, but it turned out that it wasn't. While I was lying on the floor waiting to be rescued, it dawned on me that I had locked the front door and left the key in the lock.

My mam couldn't get in. After a lot of effort trying to force the door open, she also admitted defeat. The fire brigade was called and came rushing to my aid, sirens blaring. They eventually managed to break in and help me to my feet. I ended up without a front door, but it was quite an adventure. My new door doesn't need the key to be in it to lock it from the inside, but I still have the laminate flooring. I enjoy living life on the edge.

The one that was on television. I had just won my *Britain's Got Talent* semi-final when I had a fall at the hotel bar. It had been a very long and emotional day and I just think my body had had enough. It does that sometimes. I was about to celebrate my success with my family and friends when I literally tripped over fresh air and ended up flat on my face. It did hurt quite a lot but I was more frustrated about the fact that I wasn't going to get the chance to celebrate. On the bright side, I got a lot of kisses from the D-Day Darlings, the show's brilliant wartime singing act who've since become the nation's favourites.

The one on a night out in Liverpool. I'm including this because it was quite a nasty fall, but also because I'm amazed that the mates I was out with remained friends with me afterwards. I'm not sure I'd have done the same if I was in their shoes. We were on a lads' night out. Everyone was having a great time and we were enjoying ourselves. Well, we were loving it, until I decided that it would be fun to fall over in the street and split my head open. Incidentally, it happened next to a statue of John Lennon . . . I've never listened to his music since. The hard day's night had to be cut short as my face was covered with blood and we piled into a taxi to get to a hospital, pronto. I was eventually stitched up and sent home to rest. No real lasting damage. But my mates took turns to look after me that night, making sure I'd be all right. It's entirely possible that someone even held my hand. We joke about it now but I think my friends are still traumatized by the experience. When someone hits the ground at that velocity – one second they're there next to you and the next they're on the deck – it's quite a thing.

The one in which I chipped my tooth. I was only a kid when this happened. It was just outside Argos in Consett and it wasn't the worst of falls by a long shot, but it just so happened that when I tripped, I hit my mouth on a step and chipped my front tooth. Cue a lifetime of dental treatment. Dental treatment is expensive.

The one when I went to see Frankie and the Heartstrings. I was at the Cluny in Newcastle, just about to watch Frankie and the Heartstrings perform. They're a Sunderland-based indie-rock band, but I still really like them. Once again, I fell on to a step and smashed my face in. Are you beginning to see the pattern yet? This time, I refused to go to hospital to get checked out until after the gig. I'd paid for the ticket. I'm glad I stuck around as they put on an amazing show. To salute my commitment, the band even gave me some signed merchandise afterwards. Sometimes there really is no gain without pain.

The one involving an out-of-control bike. For a change, this one isn't about me falling over nothing, like a dickhead. This is another accident that happened when I was a child and which I vividly remember because it bloody hurt. I was happily riding my bike in my parents' driveway. A three-wheeler (no two-wheeled bikes for me). I decided to go down a little hill. This felt like a good idea at the time but turned out to be a very bad one. I lost control and couldn't stop. It's a narrative you can see coming from a long way off. A normal kid would have just hit the brakes, but we've established that I'm far from normal. Instead I decided to run my bike into a wall to stop myself. Made sense at the time.

The one where I got rescued from a bathroom floor. Sadly, this isn't as kinky as it sounds. I had nipped to the toilet while I was still working for the council and the floor had just been cleaned. Over I went. I was like a turtle on its back with no chance of getting myself back up. As soon as it happened, I knew I was in the shit . . . and not because I'd fallen into the loo. I needed rescuing. I just had to decide who was going to be the rescuer. Did I want to wait for some random bloke to come into the toilet and find me on the floor (which would have looked dodgy as hell), or should I use my mobile to text my office colleagues, admit what had happened and face them joking about it for all eternity? In the end, I went for the second option and wasn't allowed to forget about it until the day I left.

HELLO? IS IT ME YOU'RE LOOKING FOR?

11

O ne of the problems of using a talker to communicate is that it's extremely hard to speak on the phone. When I call anyone for a chat, everyone always thinks I'm trying to sell them PPI and hangs up . . . even some of my own family. Trying to order gig tickets over the phone is a nightmare, especially when I go to tell them my credit-card number and it reads it as one long series of digits, which they're scrabbling to get down. I never did get those Little Mix tickets in the end . . .

Because it takes me time to type a response, the whole process tends to be very awkward. There's nothing worse than when you've waited in the queue on the telephone for an hour, and finally get through to an actual human being, only to have them cut you off before you get the chance to say hello because they can't hear you speaking and think you've hung up on them. It's a hassle, so I try to stay away from using the phone if possible.

There is, however, one advantage of using my talker on the phone. This is because I'm one of those people who see cold callers as a challenge rather than a nuisance. I really enjoy being an awkward bugger, so I've spent many hours on the line to these cold callers, trying to mess with their heads while they try in vain to sell me something.

The people who ring me up informing me that I've had an accident recently (tell me something I don't know) and that I could claim compensation are just asking for it. I don't think their training has ever prepared them for when they call a disabled bloke, who can't speak, about being involved in an accident.

'Yes, you're right,' I usually say. 'I have been involved in a nasty accident.'

The delight you hear in their voices when they hear those words could be interpreted as quite perverse and troubling, if it wasn't a sign that they've taken my bait and believe me. The gloves are off.

'Sorry to hear that, sir. Was it a car accident?' they reply.

'How did you know?' I exclaim with surprise (well, as surprised as you can sound with Graham's voice). I hook them in even further to my tall tale.

'Will you be able to help?' I continue.

'Yes, certainly, sir,' is always the reply.

Then comes the time to fuck with them. 'I was in a car accident last month and that's how I lost my voice.'

Silence usually follows while they try to process what they've just heard.

'Will you be able to help me get it back?' I add, knowing that the person at the other end now has a look of absolute panic on their face.

To give these cold callers some credit – it's a pretty tough gig, and I've done some pretty tough gigs – a few have stayed on the phone after that point and tried to continue with their scripted conversation. Most of the time, though, the phone has gone dead, and I never hear from them again. I like to think that a thick black pen strikes through my phone number, and I'm off their list once and for all.

Of course, I sometimes record these conversations for my own amusement. I say 'of course'. You might think that's strange. But I'm a comedian. Recording the laughs for future reference is part of the job description. Here's one of my favourites. I was on the phone to a guy called 'Phil' from 'Microsoft' (even though I have a Mac and 'Phil' was none the wiser). On this particular day, 'Phil' was trying to convince me I had a virus on my computer. The phone call started off professionally enough, but as time went on, 'Phil' became increasingly annoyed that I wasn't playing his game. As an aside, the reason 'Phil' is in inverted commas is because he had an Indian accent. I may be from Newcastle but I'm not falling for that one. Anyway, the phone call went something like this:

Phil: Hello . . .
Phil: Hello?
Phil: HELLO?!

Me: I can't hear you.
Phil: Can you hear me?
Me: I can't hear you.
Phil: Are you kidding with me?
Me: Sorry, I can't understand you.
Phil: I'm telling you that your computer is infected by a virus, and you don't take me seriously.
Me: That sounds terrible.
Phil: You don't take me seriously. Tell me the reason why.
Me: I can't hear you.
Phil: Fuck off! Mother-fucker, fuck off! Fuck off!
Phone goes dead.

I really hope that phone call was recorded for training purposes.

Every comedian has a list of the favourite jokes they've written. Some will be crowd-pleasers, while others are those that only the comedian finds amusing but can't bear to cut from their set (I've certainly got a few of those . . . they really *are* funny, whatever anyone else says).

I write my jokes pretty much the same way as any other comedian writes a joke. Something will trigger an idea and I'll make a note of it so I can develop it later. I have many of these notes in my phone right now. The problem is that some were written an extremely long time ago and I no longer know where they came from or what they mean. For example:

Crip Advisor – guide to places with disabled access.
My legs have been together longer than any of my relationships.
Using helium balloons to keep me upright. Not too many, though.

Anyway, if I can remember what the note is referring to, I'll get to work on expanding the idea into an actual joke. Hopefully a funny one.

I wish I was a more disciplined joke writer but I'm not. I'm far too lazy and easily distracted by *Loose Women* to sit down and write material for a whole day. I normally write my gags during short bursts of inspiration. I'd like to think I have quite a high turnover of jokes, though. It gets boring telling the same stuff over and over again. I'll use the same twenty-minute set for about six months, then gradually move on to new material, maybe sprinkling some of the new jokes alongside the old ones until I'm more comfortable with telling them. Or when the audience has obviously got bored with the old stuff. *'Have you heard the one about . . . ?' Yes, we fucking have!*

EYE PAD THEREFORE I AM

This is when my process becomes slightly different from other comedians'. Once the joke is written, I store it in my talker ready to tell in front of an audience. However, before I can tell the joke in a comedy club, I have to make sure that it sounds all right on my talker. The main problem is trying to get it to say things correctly. For example, it can't say iPad, so I have to spell it as 'eye pad'. I also have to put random punctuation in the middle of sentences to make them easier to understand when spoken out loud. There have been times when I've had to change my jokes, brilliant though they are, just because they don't sound right.

But when they work, they really work. So, in no particular order, these are ten of my favourite gags I've written:

- *If you're wondering how I got disabled, it's because I didn't forward that chain email to ten of my closest friends when I was younger.*

- *I don't always sit on a chair onstage, by the way. I just noticed that the bloke over there looks like a benefit-fraud inspector. So I'm trying to look as disabled as possible.*

- *I started off in a disabled Steps tribute band. We were called Ramps.*

- *People have often asked me why I want to put myself in a position where everyone can stare and laugh at me. The truth is that it happens to me every day anyway. At least this way there's a scheduled time and place for it.*

- *I've played the disability card so many times now that I've made an actual disability card. If I want to sit down on a busy train, I pull out the disability card. If I want tickets to a sold-out music concert, I pull out the disability card. If I see an attractive girl, who is way out of my league but obviously has a conscience and would probably sleep with me out of sympathy, I pull out more than just the disability card.*

- *As you can see, most of my jokes write themselves. But that's the beauty of auto-correct on the iPad.*

- *I am not related to Stephen Hawking in any way. However, I do hate the way people take the piss out of how he speaks. I can really synthesize with him.*

- *You probably don't recognize me from the television. I think my voice is better known than my face. Maybe it would help if I started saying phrases such as 'The next train to arrive on platform four is the 12.52 service to London King's Cross.' And, from my time at the post office, 'Please go to cashier number four.'*

- *I do actually talk in my sleep. I know I do because I always wake up with random sentences typed out on my iPad.*

- *I hate that we have so many politically correct words to describe disabled people now. I went to a school with 'spastics' in its name. They certainly knew how to make us feel good about ourselves. Now it's all special needs, special schools, special Olympics. I don't know what the fuck is so special about me. That is why it always alarms me when I hear about special forces going to war.*

Of course, a joke can seem hilarious when you write it and read it back to yourself, but the real test is whether it's a hit with the audience or not. It may surprise you to know that not all my jokes have been welcomed with open arms into the hearts and minds of the general public. Some just didn't get the reaction I thought they would. On the other hand, others have gone down a storm – and not always the ones I thought would be the real winners. The only way you can know for sure is to test your new material on the punters. That's the nerve-racking bit of the process, but it's the only way you'll find out if a joke is good enough or not. Telling it to your mam is not going to work.

WEIGHT WATCHERS IN REVERSE

It's great when people come up to me in the street, congratulate me and ask me for a selfie. It gives me a warm, fuzzy feeling and makes me feel pretty content with life. That's a big deal. It's part of what's changed in my life since winning *Britain's Got Talent*. But the whole experience has affected me physically and mentally. I'm in the public eye a lot more than I used to be. People immediately recognize me everywhere I go, and I have a lot more followers on social media. Sounds great, right? In fact, at first that was all quite hard to cope with. Mainly because I just didn't have the same amount of time to step away from my work and relax any more. We all need downtime, but now I found I was always writing new material, or booking gigs, or replying to emails. Just trying to keep on top of everything. Sometimes it all got a bit too much. I was dying to binge-watch something on Netflix and switch off completely.

After a while, I managed to adapt to the changes. For example, I used to check my social media a lot more than I do now. It was part of my daily routine. But I've learned that I can't keep on top of everything, and there's no point in beating myself up about it, so I simply don't check it as often. I've also become much better at managing my time. I plan what I need to do much more than I used to, so that everything doesn't creep up on me all at once. I used to love a deadline to galvanize me. Now I'm much better at doing things bit by bit instead of leaving them to the last moment.

My physical health is a lot harder to manage. Because I'm often travelling, I get quite tired. I have to pace myself and not push myself to do too much. Once again, I've learned to do this better recently as I've finally realized that my health is more important than my job. And if I'm not well, I can't do my job. Of course, my mam's been saying that I need to look after my health better for the last thirty-eight years. I just never used to listen to her. All good mams worry about their children's well-being – it's part of the job description. But my mam's worried more than most for obvious reasons.

She's always been particularly watchful about my weight. I've never really weighed very much. And I'm one of those lucky people who can eat anything they like and not get any heavier, which is fortunate, given my love of cakes and sweets. My mam definitely saw this inability to gain weight, particularly when I was younger, as more of a challenge than a blessing. She was a bit of a feeder, always trying to get me to eat something. She would feed me, then immediately weigh me to see if I'd put on any weight. Most kids have one of those height charts so they can show how tall they've grown. I didn't have one of those. I had a weight chart instead to plot how fat I had become. The fatter the better. It was like going to Weight Watchers but in reverse. If I managed to put weight on, I got a gold star, but if I didn't I'd have to go back for second helpings. This system came to an abrupt end when I was about twelve, because I tried to weigh my pet black Labrador and broke the scales.

At times in my life I've hated being the one who's different. I've found myself asking, 'Why can't I just be like everyone else?' Because I felt like this, I used to try my very best not to look disabled. I refused to use a wheelchair. I refused to eat in public because everyone would see me making a mess. I refused help from other people because I saw that as admitting defeat. It's been tough. One of the worst aspects of my condition is the dribbling. I can't control my swallowing so there's almost always a constant stream of saliva coming from my gob. Attractive, right? I've learned to cope with it over the years. I carry tissues everywhere with me to wipe my chin when I need to (which is awkward in itself: imagine what the cleaner thinks when they find loads of used tissue in my hotel room). And I often take a change of clothes if I'm going anywhere just in case something gets marked. A key bit of dribbler's insider knowledge is the trick of wearing a striped top if you don't want the marks to show up. But it's still probably the most embarrassing part of my disability, and seems like the thing people notice most.

I'm very self-conscious about whether I'm dribbling or not, especially onstage with all those faces watching me. Do you remember that big dog you once met that drooled all over your face at a party? Well, I'm the human version. I can't tell you how awkward it is when I go to hug a mate and end up getting saliva all over his clean shirt. And it gives a whole new meaning to drooling over nice girls.

I've tried to stop it happening. I've had a few operations to re-route my salivary glands, which didn't fix the problem, and I've also had hyoscine patches put behind my ears – they work by drying up the saliva in your mouth. If anything, these worked too well because they dried me up so much that I started to have blurred vision. I was told that my mouth was dry – I just couldn't see the results.

But the way I feel about myself has changed since *Britain's Got Talent*. I've become more comfortable with my disability. I didn't notice it at first – it just sort of crept up on me. Then one day I was riding around in my mobility scooter and realized

I didn't care if I looked disabled any more. I was fine with driving a scooter (though everyone I've crashed into might question that assessment). When I realized I felt differently about myself, I started thinking about other things I'm more comfortable with. I'm a lot more at ease with using my talker. In the past, it used to stress me out when I had to speak to new people because I knew they wouldn't know what to expect. I felt under pressure to type faster so I could reply sooner, to keep the conversation flowing. It was almost as if my using a talker was an inconvenience to them and I had to answer quickly so that I wasn't wasting their time. But now I feel differently. I don't care if I take a bit longer to reply. A lot of people have seen me use my talker so I assume they're used to it and understand the experience. But added to that, I just feel more confident in myself as a whole.

People often ask me what the best thing was about winning the show. Was it the £250,000 prize money, or the chance to perform in front of the Royal Family? Well, I'd love to answer that question but, according to the new Apple Watch I'm wearing right now, it's time to drive my Porsche to the airport, and get on my private jet to Monte Carlo. I'm joking, of course. As if I'd drive myself to the airport!

In fact, the best thing is that, for the first time in my life, I'm actually proud to be disabled. I'm not embarrassed. I'm not disappointed. I'm not angry. And that makes me feel great.

'Can I have a go?'

Obviously I don't mind when my friends type on my talker because they're just having a bit of fun, but it's surprising how many random strangers try to type on it as well. Drunk people are especially guilty of this. They'll happily take my talker off me in a bar and start typing away on it. I'm sure you can guess what the most popular words they get it to say are. 'Fuck', 'bastard' and 'bollocks' are all on the leaderboard. To be fair, UK Adult Male Graham does a particularly good job with swear words. But I often wonder how they'd feel if I suddenly ripped their vocal cords out of their throats and started playing with them. Just for a laugh.

One of my favourite things is when random people see my talker, ask me what it's for, and then say how they wish they had one too. 'Yes, mate, it's great having to rely on a machine to chat for you. It's the best thing in the world!' Funnily enough, they're not as keen on the idea when I offer to swap my talker for their voice.

Because lots of random people type a lot of random shit on my talker (and also because I'm a comedian who types a lot of random shit anyway), my predictive text is pretty fucked up. I use two apps to speak on my talker at the moment, Proloquo2Go and Proloquo4Text, and both predict my sentences based on what I've said in the past. Currently on the predicted sentence list is:

- Hello, how are you?
- Thank you
- Thanks very much
- Have a nice day
- I'm good, thanks
- Please lick me

That last one is a line from my Radio 4 sitcom, *Ability*, and does not indicate my sexual preferences in any way. What with one thing and another, I said it a lot during the recording of the show and now it's stuck with me for ever.

These pre-programmed phrases – various greetings, as well as stuff like my address and phone number – come in very useful at times, especially when I'm dying for the toilet and my hands can't type fast enough to ask where it is. I can just hit one button, ask the question and avoid pissing my pants. You're probably all jealous that you can't do the same with your actual voice. We'd all save a lot of time if we didn't have to think about what we were going to say next. Imagine having a bunch of chat-up lines all ready to go when you meet a nice lass or lad without having to think about it. Basically, it's my equivalent of copying and pasting messages on dating websites. It's been pretty successful so far . . . as long as I don't say, 'Please lick me,' by accident.

The fact that my talker remembers everything I've ever said also means that auto-correct can be a ducking nightmare too. This usually happens at the most awkward of times. I'm pretty sure my talker has a mind of its own and does this on purpose. For example, I once asked a girl if she had a pen I could borrow so that I could write down her number. I didn't expect it to say, 'Can I borrow your penis?' She was a little surprised too.

My ex-girlfriend and I once got thrown out of a paint shop when I said I wanted to defecate in the living room. But the worst of all was when I got some chewing gum stuck in my hair. I asked my girlfriend's mother if she knew how to get it out. Sadly, my talker decided to say, 'Do you know how to get cum out of my hair?' It got even more awkward when she knew exactly what to do.

Despite all of these operational issues, using a talker has its advantages. For example, when I can't be arsed to talk to someone who's being really annoying, I can just pretend my batteries are dead. Is that rude? Or would you do exactly the same thing sometimes if you had the opportunity?

I'm not sure why so many people act so idiotically around disabled people. In most cases, I don't think it's intentional or that anything negative is meant by it. No one wants to be an idiot, right, and most people don't set out to be. It just happens. People simply don't know how to act when they meet someone different from them.

I think we're all guilty of this. People are so used to whatever their concept of normal human interaction is that when someone different comes along they're thrown. They're not used to a bloke who can't communicate in the usual way, and who they can't really read. They're not getting the well-versed social signs through body language and facial expression, so they're not sure how they're doing. *Am I saying the right things? Am I keeping eye contact in the right way? Should I be more serious or less serious? Is it time to break into my song-and-dance routine?*

In a way, this puts me at a great advantage, because I have control of the situation, simply because the other person hasn't experienced anything like it before, and I have, every day of my life. Therefore they're probably going to follow my lead. I've gone from having a massive disadvantage to having the upper hand.

Not that I necessarily know how to make the best of this temporary reversal of fortune. It probably doesn't help that I'm the most socially awkward person in the world, even at the best of times. Despite what you may see on stage or on the television – you know, the smooth, cool guy who owns the room – the reality is that what you see is not necessarily what you get. Everyone likes to think that their life will end up happily ever after, with a relationship, and a family, and everything else that goes with that. And why not? But I honestly believe that I won't. I'm not cut out for all of that stuff. I'd just mess it up anyway.

Can you imagine me trying to raise a child? For a start, I'd probably just name my kid 'One' so that I could call them in for tea very quickly on my talker. I wouldn't be able to help teach my lucky offspring to talk and I'd probably keep dropping him or her on the floor. If I can't be trusted to look after my talker without breaking it, then I definitely shouldn't be given responsibility for a child. So, I'm happy to settle for what I have. My point is that maybe I'm not helping myself. How can I expect other people to treat me normally when I don't really think of myself as normal?

I'm putting the blame for any awkwardness I experience firmly on being British. It's a radical thought, I know, but maybe us Brits are just too uptight about stuff. We're too embarrassed to admit when we don't understand something, and too polite to ask the questions that would help us to figure it out. Instead we just make the whole situation worse by saying the wrong thing. Or, even worse, saying nothing. *Something awkward's happening. I'll just keep quiet and hope it goes away.* Many awkward problems seem so uniquely British that it's no wonder we can't get 'how to do disabled' right.

As a nation, we can't even ask a person to repeat themselves more than three times without laughing it off, pretending we caught what they said and hoping for the best. We can't see a friend in the supermarket without creeping around the aisles to make sure we never make eye contact again. And we have a habit of refusing to change direction in the street suddenly without first looking at our phone and pretending to frown at it, as though it's the phone's fault rather than our own idiocy that we're going the wrong way.

Back when I had my proper job, in an office and everything, the woman on reception thought my name was Danny. As ever, I thought I'd just let it go. Then it happened again. And again. And again.

'Morning, Danny!'

'How are you today, Danny?'

'You're late again, Danny.'

She thought my name was Danny for six years. All because it had got too awkward for me to correct her. She even signed my leaving card 'Good luck, Dan', despite everyone else using my real name, right there in black and white. I'll never be a 'Don't you know who I am?' person but, seriously, didn't she know who I was?

So, if anything, I'm helping to keep the circle of awkwardness going by not putting people straight. *Do you need some help? Yes, please, I'd love you to help me across the road. What's it like living with cerebral palsy? Oh, no trouble at all, thanks.* I'm British. I was brought up not to make a fuss and just get on with things. Even if it means letting people take my iPad from me and talking to me with it, typing away, because they think I'm deaf as well as unable to speak.

These stupid moments of unease occur because we, as a population, haven't been educated enough. It is just in recent years that disabled people have become more visible in society. The most obvious example of a high-profile disabled person, and probably the one who was in the public eye longest, was Stephen Hawking. But there are many others as well: RJ Mitte (who played Walt Junior in *Breaking Bad*), comedian Francesca Martinez (formerly a star of the school drama *Grange Hill*) and James Moore (currently starring in the British soap *Emmerdale*). The reason I mention these three in particular is because in their recent on-screen roles their disabilities were hardly mentioned. They were just another character in a television programme. That shows how much progress can be made if we really want it to happen.

Before all this, disabled people didn't really have a voice so there are still generations who haven't grown up with disabled people integrated into society. Perhaps it isn't fair, then, to expect them to understand how to treat disabled people if they have had no experience of them. We have to get away from the idea of disabled people being wildly different or being a problem in society, in exactly the same way that views on other minority groups have changed over the years. I'd like to think that the younger generations are growing up with more disabled people in the public eye, and as they see them leading a perfectly normal life, they won't bat an eyelid. Hopefully these people will grow up with a better understanding and acceptance of disabilities. In a hundred years' time, maybe we'll look back at these stupid questions and be amazed that they were ever asked. I hope so.

I've had first-hand experience of facing an audience who weren't sure about the disabled bloke onstage at the start of the night. *Am I allowed to laugh? Should I feel sorry for him? Where the hell is his carer?* But by the end of the night they'd forgotten all of that awkwardness and social anxiety and were just enjoying someone telling jokes for a living. I won't mention the time I got asked after a gig if I was a character act . . . Suffice to say, some people are beyond help.

And that's why I'd like to see more disabled comedians booked by comedy clubs, appearing at festivals and being shown on television – more disabled people being portrayed in a positive light. I'm sick of being part of a group in society who are mostly demonized in the media (unless they can win a shiny medal, of course). That's exactly why hate crimes against the disabled are on the rise.

Success breeds success. It would be nice for every disabled child to realize they have the opportunity to do whatever they like when they grow up. But they'll only believe this if they see other people in a similar situation achieving their goals. The comedy scene can play a big part in this. And comedy is the perfect way to tackle difficult subjects: it can make people laugh *and* think. Programmes like *The Last Leg* on Channel 4 have paved the way for a new perspective on disability, but there's still a lot that could be done. Only when we see disabled people on our stages and on our screens as much as anyone else will attitudes really change. And only then will disabled people feel fully a part of society. As a comedian, I hope that the industry I work in can be at the forefront of changing people's attitudes.

I've always seen the funny side of my disability. If I
didn't laugh about it, then I'd definitely cry. And I've
always used that humour as a defence mechanism. If I
could laugh at myself that meant no one could laugh at
me. It helped take some of the stigma away from being
different. So when you look at it from that point of
view, maybe it's not all that surprising that it was
through comedy that I eventually found my voice.

Afterwords

THE VOICE OF THE DISABLED OFFERS SOME LIFE HACKS

Right now, whenever anyone in the media wants the view of a disabled person on a certain subject, I'll inevitably get a phone call asking for a comment. I'm not exactly sure who decided on this. I'm assuming that all disabled people met up and took a vote but, if that's the case, then I wasn't invited to cast mine. If I'd had a vote, I would have chosen someone much more responsible than me. I'm far too silly to carry the title 'Voice of the Disabled' on my already very weak shoulders. Nevertheless, I'm not the kind of person who shirks their responsibilities. So, as the representative of blue-badge holders everywhere, I have some requests. On behalf of all of us.

With immediate effect, and in no particular order, we would like to ban:

1. Buttons. They're the devil's handiwork. Especially when I'm dying for a wee and can't unfasten my jeans quickly enough. I've lost count of the number of pairs of Levi's I've ruined. I have one word for you: Velcro. It's the future! It's been around since the fifties, of course, but it's still the future.

2. Jeans. Why do we need jeans? What place is there for them in the world? Not only can I not unfasten them, I can't even take them off without struggling for half an hour. Sartorial standards aside, tracksuit bottoms are so much easier.

3. Laces. I refer you to the above point about Velcro.

4. The countdown clock at pedestrian crossings. You have no idea of the pressure they put me under. They usually start counting when I'm only halfway across and for me it's like a countdown to imminent death.

5. Standing ovations. A bit of a piss-take if you're in a wheelchair.

6. Tightly wrapped sweets. I've started to eat Starbursts with the paper still on. Needs must.

7. Stairs. Just no.

8. Those special keys needed to gain access to public disabled toilets. That's right! You need a magic key to open an accessible public toilet. I'm no good with keys at the best of times, never mind when I'm bursting for the toilet. And let's not get started on the fact that I still have to lock the door once I'm inside. The light will probably be off as well so I have to locate that in the darkness, then struggle for half an hour with my jeans. But the key question is why they're called 'disabled toilets' when there's nothing wrong with them.

9. Cobbled streets. When I'm going along a cobbled street in my wheelchair, it feels like I'm on a truly crap theme-park ride. If I wanted that experience, I'd just go to Lightwater Valley. I'm pretty sure that cobbles were invented just to keep disabled people from going anywhere.

10. Hills. Everywhere should be flat and easy to walk around. I'm looking at you, Edinburgh.

11. Accessible hotel rooms with baths instead of show-ers. Why would you give me an accessible room with a wider doorway, lower bed and roughly a million emergency cords for me to pull, but then make it impossible for me to have a wash? If you ever meet me and I smell less than fragrant, I've probably just had a night in one of these rooms. I apologize for the stink.

12. Guide dogs. Why should blind people be allowed their own animal when I can't have a talking parrot?

13. Television programmes for the hard of hearing that are shown at 3 a.m. The only people who are up at that time are Uber drivers and murderers, none of whom are likely to be in the market for a signed show.

When you've lived with a disability for thirty-eight years, you tend to pick up a few tips and tricks along the way that help make life easier. I like to call these 'disabled life hacks' and they have become essential to helping me live my life, so as a parting gift I thought I'd share the best ones:

1. A trouser-hanger can hold open your book. If you have trouble holding your book when you're reading, just pop it into a trouser-hanger and let that do the hard work for you. No more losing your page in the middle of an exciting story.

2. Oh dear, you've dropped something and you can't bend down and pick it up without toppling over and ending up in Accident and Emergency. Again. Never fear, the solution is simple. Just use some hair-straighteners to retrieve said object from the floor. Make sure they're turned off, though.

3. Remember that, when having a drink, size matters. Next time you order a drink at your favourite cafe or fast-food joint, you may want to try asking for your drink in a cup the next size up. A small latte in a medium-size cup makes it easier to carry without spilling. Ta-dah!

4. As a comedian, I'm always on the road and I find myself in a lot of service stations. I even have a list of

my favourites (Tebay is top). Anyway, the problem is that I'm not very good at eating fast food from these places. It's always too chewy or difficult to shove down my throat in the short amount of time I have. I've found the solution, though. Just buy a ready meal from the shop at the services and stick it in the microwaves that these places always have available. Technically, they're there for customers to heat up baby food, but who's going to notice?

5. Carry a water bottle everywhere. I got sick and tired of always spilling my drinks over myself while I was out with mates, or needing somebody else to hold my drink the entire time. I had to come up with a practical solution, but I couldn't quite figure it out. Then one day I saw my friend take a sports water bottle to the gym and realized that water bottles weren't just for water. Now I bring my water bottle everywhere, and pour almost any kind of drink into it.

6. Prosthetic limbs to help you get legless. I've learned from personal experience that a mate's prosthetic arm or leg makes for an excellent receptacle if you're clean out of cups.

7. Whether you're eating in, or taking out, always order your food to go. Takeaway packaging is a lot easier to carry, whether you're on wheels or just have trouble balancing. You can also always ask for a bag for your food, which may help too, and saves you looking like a greedy pig because you don't have to ask for a doggy bag for your leftovers. You're welcome.

8. Scarves make great bibs. Whatever the weather, it's always worth rocking some kind of scarf or other neck accessory with your outfit, not because scarves are fashionable but because they're totally practical. I almost always wear one if I know I'm out to dinner, because if it gets messy I can just take it off and the rest of my outfit is still clean. On the downside, you will look like a bit of a hipster.

9. It's good to talk. If you're struggling to figure out how to do something, there's no better person to ask than somebody else living with a disability. Although we're all affected a little differently, and everyone has their own way of doing things, somebody else's little hack can often be a life-changer. I am so grateful to the other people with cerebral palsy who have helped me figure out how to hack my way through life with a disability.

Acknowledgements

This book would not have been possible without my amazing and very patient editor, Andrea Henry, and her fantastic team at Transworld, especially Hannah Bright and Alice Murphy-Pyle. Thank you for giving me the opportunity to write these words.

A huge amount of appreciation has to go to Ben Thompson for helping me kick my words into shape. His insight and advice was invaluable during the writing process.

I'd also like to thank my agents, Andrew Roach, Lee Martin, and everyone else at Andrew Roach Talent and Gag Reflex, for helping me to get to where I am today. You were right, auditioning for *Britain's Got Talent* was a good idea, after all!

Thanks to my literary agent, Diana Beaumont, for being the voice of calm and reason when my deadlines were fast approaching.

I'm also very grateful to Paul Sullivan for helping to keep me in the limelight long enough to write this book.

Special recognition goes to my teachers, Mr Pod and Mrs Fraser, for realizing I had a bright future and making me believe in myself. And, of course, to all my family for letting me follow this crazy dream of mine.

Finally, a massive thanks to Nathan Wood, who convinced me to try stand-up comedy in the first place. Cheers for being a great mate. I'll always be in your debt.

SCOPE = Equality for disabled people

Scope exists to achieve a society where all disabled people enjoy equality and fairness. We're a strong community of disabled and non-disabled people. We provide practical and emotional information and support when it's needed most. We use our collective power to change attitudes and end injustice. And we campaign relentlessly to create a fairer society. We are so grateful to Lee for being a Disability Gamechanger and for his invaluable support in helping Scope end inequality for disabled people.

'It's an honour to be an Ambassador for such a great charity. It has helped me and so many other disabled people over the years, and it's a pleasure to now work so closely with them. Together I hope that we can support a lot of other disabled people to achieve whatever they want in life in the future.'

Lee Ridley

For more information please visit www.scope.org.uk

About the Author

Lee Ridley is also known as Lost Voice Guy. He is a stand-up comedian, writer and tech geek based in Newcastle upon Tyne. Lee developed cerebral palsy as a baby and communicates using an iPad. A bit like Stephen Hawking. Though, in Lee's words, better looking. He is a BBC New Comedy Award winner, his Radio 4 sitcom *Ability* has had two series and counting, and he is the winner of 2018's *Britain's Got Talent*. Lee has appeared on *Live at the Apollo* and at the *Royal Variety Performance*, sold out at the Edinburgh Fringe and had his first nationwide tour in 2019. He is an ambassador for Scope. *I'm Only In It for the Parking* is his first book.